LAO ZI
PHILOSOPHY
— of —
LIBERAL
GOVERNMENT

Prof. Chung Boon Kuan, PhD

PARTRIDGE

A Penguin Random House Company

To order additional copies of this book, contact
Toll Free 800 101 2657 (Singapore)
Toll Free 1 800 81 7340 (Malaysia)
orders.singapore@partridgepublishing.com

www.partridgepublishing.com/singapore

DEDICATION

To my lovely wife, Sheau Wen, who finds passion in

the Philosophy of Lao Zi and be liberated

through the English translation

Non-intervention and Righteousness are the guiding principles of the
Chinese Emperors in governing the Middle Kingdom.

"The Taoists were the world's first libertarians, who believed in virtually no interference by the state in economy or society."—Murray N. Rothbard, *Economic Thought Before Adam Smith*

The world is full of debates on who is right and who is wrong. If an idea is absolutely right, there will be no doubt about it and need no debate. If an idea is absolutely wrong, it cannot stand the test of the history and need no debate as well. Upon reading Tao Te Jing, if you are still bounded by man-made social norms, troubled by what is right and what is wrong, scared by myths, addicted to ineffective policy, no conviction to the Law of Nature or Tao, you have been sleepwalking. On the other hand, if you become wild, bewildered and not knowing what is best for you and your family, assume you can live without others, no regard for man-made laws, you may consider living in a jungle.

CONTENTS

PREFACE

"Lao Zi Philosophy of Liberal Government" is a book written for the people and their government. Although Tao Te Jing is an ancient philosophical work, and the world has become much more liberal compared to the past centuries, its philosophical values to build and govern a country are still relevant and important for the people and their leaders to understand.

Tao Te Jing was written in an ancient poetic form which was very different from the modern Chinese language. This book is a translation and commentary from the perspective of the original intention of Tao Te Jing. However, since Lao Zi advocated harmonizing with the Great Nature, there are unlimited concepts that we can learn from it and apply it in everything we do. After all, we do need to govern our body, family, organization, if not the country.

The author uses insights learned from his engineering background to interpret how different things affect our world and what we should do based on the philosophy of Lao Zi. The author tries to extract the fundamental principles of the philosophy and make them easier to understand and apply, as opposed to other interpretations in history and direct translations to other languages which have a strong inclination towards literary form. In particular, it demonstrates the needs to learn from the One Law of Nature, or Tao, to justify the validity and survivability of those principles of which the Great Nature has walked the walk and proven to us through its longevity. The Great Nature does not need to talk. It leads by examples and it gains our trust through its deeds.

The natural order of the Great Nature is one which favors free-market systems but does not confine to economics aspect. Freedom is the most precious to everybody. One who lives without freedom, including freedom of the mind, does not really have a life. We have been educated to obey the norms, to believe in what the State want us to believe since they control our education system, making our minds fixated with bias views and see reality as being divided in the preference of certain groups. It produces individuals who are addicted to power, money, fame, drugs, gambling, racing, and all sorts of things which lead to chaos and unsatisfied lives. And addicts have different tastes and views about their lives and of others. We have to change our mindset. But, if the mind is set, how can it be changed? After a biscuit is baked, how can we reshape it? The answer is: we must crush it; add in some water and baking powder, make it into any shape we want; and then bake it again. It is commonsense. The same answer applies to changing mindset. The mind must first be made flexible and be free to accept new ideas; be convinced of the real truth; and embrace it as a new way of life.

The first step of becoming flexible and free is vital. The rise of Japan started with a near-total discard of their tradition during the Meiji Revolution.

Another feature of this book is that it is based on the original Tao Te Jing from archeological discoveries out of ancient tombs in 1973 and 1993. It explains the philosophy of Lao Zi based on the fundamental principles of Lao Zi. It is unlike other interpretations in history which are based on the common version widely available that has more than 140 errors compared to the original literature. The errors were knowingly made by pseudo-intellects and scholars in history with fixated minds of Confucius teachings. They were not able to understand some of the extraordinary concepts of Lao Zi and they took the liberty to change the original text into the sentences that they can then explain with their logic.

Non-intervention and Righteousness advocated by Lao Zi have been used as the guiding principles of the Chinese Emperors in governing the Middle Kingdom during the glorious periods. Non-intervention doesn't mean one doesn't care. It is like parents watching their adult children but do nothing, absolutely nothing, unless there is something to do. Have faith in them and give them total freedom to make good decisions as well as bad ones. Just because we have a just cause doesn't mean we have the rights and responsibilities to impose our desires on our children. We must not try to be clever and assume we know which way to go because there is a chance we may be pushing them in the wrong direction but we are overconfident to overlook the obvious. Step aside and trust in nature, life will find a way.

True love is manifested in wanting our love ones to have total freedom.

Independence is freedom. But independence literally means depending on no one. So, one is free when one is self-reliant. The independence of a country is truly attained when the people need not depend on the government to take care of their economic and social needs; and the government can manage its country without colonial rule. The people will protect their country, for their self interest, and not relying on the government to do the job. They must instead remind themselves not to let the dangerous government machinery be abused by corrupted officers and destroy the country.

Unity leads to stupidity; diversity and freedom lead to innovation. Many problems are created due to human desires for control or to do some ambitious things. The world will be a better place when a sustainable mutual understanding is developed between the people and the government. The understanding is: the people do not like to be interfered, whether the intervention is benevolence or otherwise; and the government does not like to intervene. The mandate of the government is: to control the legalized forces in protecting the lives and properties of the people; and to manage the assets of the country. Therefore, this book is a reference for both the people and the government to facilitate this mutual understanding so that no people will ask for more and no politicians will do more than required. No politicians can get away with exploiting the weakness of some voters by offering pretentious generosity and filthy lucre bait, out of national resources and debt, to fish for votes and take advantage over rival parties. The governments are responsible for the current social and economic problems in the world due to their unwarranted use of "cleverness" or pseudo-intellectual to intervene in almost everything. But they arrogantly represent themselves as the cure. And the people believe it and want the interventions. That makes the people guilty of collective conspiracy and rightly to share some responsibilities. There is no hope until the psychology of the average people change.

INTRODUCTION

Lao Zi wrote a book around 500 B.C., at the onset of the Warring States Period, and it is commonly known as "Tao Te Jing". It was written to express his philosophy of how a king should govern his country. It covers the fundamental concepts of learning from the Great Nature, spiritual well-being and attitude of the king, civil liberty, educating the people not to rely on the government, national defense and military strategies. It was used explicitly by the emperors of the early Han Dynasty as the guiding principles to govern the country. Its various concepts were also applied by many other emperors in the subsequent dynasties in Chinese history. It has since been elaborated from different perspectives and used in applications which deviate from its original intention. For example, a group of people who believe in deities and ghosts has applied it to re-brand their religion, called Taoism today, by making Lao Zi one of their deities. They also applied certain verses of Tao Te Jing in their spiritual practice thinking that they will be able to elevate themselves to become deities as well. However, the book has been widely used by scholars in history as a "medicine" to heal their broken hearts or as guidance for spiritual well-being. Some people, including Mao Ze Dong, have used the book as a complement to Sun Zi Art of War in devising military strategies. These are no surprises as philosophical thoughts can usually be applied in many aspects. Sun Zi has been used not only in war but also in business, biomedical, etc. Since Lao Zi advocated harmonizing with the Great Nature, there are unlimited concepts that we can learn from it and apply in everything we do. After all, we need to govern our body, family, organization, if not the country.

There are many uncommon or anti-norm ideas in Tao Te Jing. Many people, including myself, may have ditched the book upon reading those "wacky" ideas. But as one gains more social experience or has a broken heart due to over-ambitious, having too much self-esteem, over-religious, over-passionate, etc, he or she will be able to understand and appreciate the book better. It is all because we are so bounded by norms and cannot jump out of the unnecessary restrictions. Lao Zi teaches us to break free from those norms, to keep an open mind for no rules are absolutely right or absolutely wrong, not to hate the negative notions like ugly, immoral, cowed, unintelligent, useless etc. because they are just relative measurements and the words existed due to the bias perceptions of human, often controlled by the dominant groups, influencing us to think that something is good and the opposite is bad in the preference of those groups. For example, when a famous beautician says that skinny girls are beautiful, many girls will fast to be skinny and feel bad if they couldn't meet the standard. If one day the beautician says that fat ladies are beautiful, many ladies will then put on weight. Are you stupid to follow the trend? Yes and no. Yes in one perspective and no in another perspective. In terms of useful and useless, you become useless when you refuse to be used. So, being useless is wise.

Lao Zi teaches us to learn from the Nature. More rain falls in location A and less in location B is not because the Nature is dearer to the people in location A, or the other way around. The Nature has no feeling. It does what it does to nurture all lives and it doesn't care whether it is appreciated or not. It gives what it can afford, like a routine, and doesn't force itself to give more. It cares for everything but doesn't get emotionally attached to anything. It doesn't have a body or form, it is nothingness. If it has feeling of love and hate, it will get old like all forms of life. So, a country which tries to become a welfare state will go on a road to bankruptcy. The people must rely on themselves rather than on the government. According to Lao

Zi, the best government is one that the people know it existed but doesn't feel its interference (minimum tax, minimum regulation, and minimum welfare). The second best government is one that the people love and praise it. The third is the government that the people fear. And the worst is the government that the people hate and despise.

In the history of China, government was not synonymous to politics. In fact, political parties were undesirable or prohibited. Members of the government were given the freedom to discuss and debate matters of policy and direction, like members of one big family. Different opinions were accommodated in the belief that they can be harmonized because everybody was working for the common cause as opposed to survival of any party. (This is similar to Leninist's Democratic Centralism consisted of "freedom of discussion, unity of action.") Everyone must agree to disagree after a decision has been made. Sabotage would amount to disloyalty to the emperor who supposedly represented the God to take care of everything in this world. If the plan didn't work, those who suggested the brilliant idea would have to bear the responsibility, not the emperor. The emperor merely gave the opportunity and trust for those individuals to try out their ideas. If the idea worked, they must instead thank the emperor rather than claim victory or credit for themselves. So, is it good to be ambitious, both in the part of the emperor and the ministers? The philosophy of government is righteous, not conspiracy or battling to gain power. According to Lao Zi, it is not wise to gain power and you must be wise when you have the power. One would be the leader only if everybody wants him to be the leader and he has no choice, in a way forced to do national service rather than to let idiots ruin the country.

There are fundamental differences between governing a country and managing a company. The leader of a country is to protect the people (i.e. law enforcement and defense against external enemies), and give them the freedom to do what they wish for their well-being and prosperity. The wealth of a nation is distributed and held by the people, not the government. On the contrary, the wealth of a company belongs to the shareholders. Many businessmen would squeeze every drop out of their employees or maximize profit out of their customers. The major portion of the profit is kept by the directors who often hold the lion shares and enjoy exceptional pays and privileges. The promise of bonuses is just the trivial trickle down and bait under the pretext that more profit to the company equals more benefit to the employees. Businessmen often dare to take risks offensively in bet for greater returns. As a country leader, one should "dare not" take risks. He should only take risks defensively to safeguard the country. He should not aim to become hero of war or social welfare, because this will mean more tax on the people and also put the people at risk of physical and financial hurts. He should not heed the call for deficit spending from rich businessmen whom greed can never be satisfied. Building infrastructure may not necessarily be a good investment if it is not productivity-enhancing but merely a white elephant to provide temporary lifeline to certain groups. He should have the courage to dare-not do too much, although he might be disliked and blamed for not being "productive" by the standard of certain people who crave for charity from the government. After all, the measurement of productivity varies with perspectives of different people. We are so small and insignificant compared to the ocean, the earth, and the universe. We will still be negligibly small no matter how much we feel proud of ourselves.

Tao Te Jing was written in an ancient poetic form which was very different from the modern Chinese language. The writing style of Lao Zi is, he likes to start each philosophical verse by describing the behavior of the Great Nature (including the universe, water, wind, etc.) before he continues to say how we should learn from that. There exist many versions of interpretation in Chinese literatures of different times in history, each with different understanding and perceptions of the writers. There are a few direct translations to English but they are all based on the copy which has more than 140 errors compared to the original literature. With the archeological discoveries of copies of the original literature retrieved from ancient tombs in 1973 and 1993, coupled with the crises happening around the world, I suddenly feel a renewed interest in Tao Te Jing because it offers many answers to what actually go wrong with the world. The present text is my version of translation, in simple English. I hope it provides some useful new ideas to the readers. As Lao Zi suggested, never take the words of anyone at face value. Even his original thoughts may be questioned. Tao that is described by anyone is not the true Tao. We must be wise in making our own judgment on what is the best way of conduct at different time and space.

Some of the basic concepts of Lao Zi are:

1. Tao can only be learnt and cannot be taught. Knowledge can be transferred but intellect can only be learnt by the individual himself. Tao is close to the Law of Nature. Don't talk too much on what is Tao because the more we talk the more it will deviate from the true Tao as we become fixated with perceptions. (道法自然，知者不言)

2. Don't argue what is right and what is wrong. Right in one case may be wrong in another scenario. Use Tao as the guiding principle. Recognize that a balance of Ying and Yang (or opposite polarities) is essential. Be accommodative, in terms of ideas and behaviors. (道无常，有无相生)

3. Love all people unconditionally and do not expect any return. Be generous to people of all kinds, no preference; give if you think you ought to, are able, willing and ready to give. Never burden yourself with responsibility of the life and death of other people. Everybody is to rely on himself and never expect any charity from others, much less the government. This is the foundation of personal liberty. Don't control the people. Give everybody the freedom to make good decisions as well as bad ones. Love all things but don't assume you have the right to dictate the fate of anybody for any "just cause" that you may have. (慈而不仁，长而弗宰)

4. Be thrifty, emotionally and financially. No big desire, therefore there is no need for big spending. No big ambition. No obsessive

favor or dislike. Not too much cheer and not too much grief. Waste nothing if we choose to live in harmony with the Nature. Resources are limited. Affections are also limited. If one wishes to extend the same affection for his first child to every subsequent offspring, he will collapse when he has ten or more children. "Got to be cruel to be kind, in the right measure." (俭，无欲)

5. Use soft approach. Pretend to be weak. Take no confrontational stand. The military is only meant for national defense. Don't be arrogant to fight for world leadership role. Have the courage to dare-not go to war and resist instigations to become a superpower. Forbear offenses and provocations as much as possible. (柔而不争，不敢为天下先)

6. Don't overlook the importance of nothingness. Empty space within a bottle is what makes the bottle useful. Don't fill it up. Don't strive for perfection and becomes an extremist. At the same time, don't feel contented but keep learning. Stay hungry, stay foolish. (无之用，用之不盈)

7. Don't be greedy/egoistic/obsessive in accumulating any kind of personal achievement and glory. Do ordinary, natural, not-ambitious work instead. Don't intervene unnecessarily. When there is no expectation of any government intervention, the people will build up their ability to deal with any problems they face and help themselves. Have faith in a free market system. (寡欲无为，上德不德)

8. The government and the people are inter-dependent. The government will not exist without the people, and their support thereof. The people are not inferior to the government, the people are not fed by the government, and the government is not the nanny of the people. The government is made up of members of the nation paid to manage the legalized force to protect the properties of the people and uphold their liberty. Everybody, including the leader, has a genuine self-interest in the economy, wealth equality, and social justice of the country. (天地不自生，贵大患若身)

9. Do what is necessary to care for the people but don't expect anything in return. Claim no credit for any success because it is not the work of a single person and decision could be made because of the trust of the people. (为而弗恃 成功而弗居)

10. No preference and no indifference towards brilliant individuals. Don't be opportunistic and try to use clever tricks. Learn everything around us but don't aim to use the knowledge. (不上贤, 绝圣弃知, 明白四达 能毋以知乎)

The republic system is implicitly advocated by Lao Zi, although he does not reject the monarchy system. In a country of the people, by the people and for the people, the people's rights are more important than the country because the country is simply a piece of hardware. The people will protect their country like maintaining their house, but no people shall be sacrificed just because some leaders decided to "beautify" the country the way they wanted without considering the feelings of some stakeholders who want it other ways. The President is just one of the people, so he is not more superior than the people. He is hired by the people to do the job. There must be a mutual understanding between the people and the government. The understanding is: the people do not like to be interfered, whether the intervention is benevolence or otherwise; and the government does not like to intervene. The mandate of the government is: to control the legalized forces in protecting the lives and properties of the people; and to manage the assets of the country. Therefore, this book is a reference for both the people and the government to facilitate this mutual understanding so that no people will ask for more and no politicians will do more than required. No politicians can get away with exploiting the weakness of some voters by offering pretentious generosity and filthy lucre bait, out of national resources and debt, to fish for votes and take advantage over rival parties. In a democratic country, the elected representatives are no better than winners of beauty contests; i.e. they are elected based on their appealing looks and sweet-talking styles. They are not really smart individuals. But they arrogantly represent themselves as the wise guys. Due to their unwarranted use of "cleverness" or pseudo-intellect to intervene in almost everything, the governments created the various social and economic problems in the world today. Since the people have the expectation that the government always has to do something to worth their pays, albeit the lack of competency, and want the interventions anyway, that makes the people guilty of collective conspiracy and rightly to share some responsibilities too. There is no hope until the psychology of the average people change.

This book is written for all the people of the world who care about personal liberty and pay attention to politics and governance. The reader will learn the philosophy of Lao Zi which emphasizes giving freedom to all the people for the self-interest of every individuals as well as the collective interest of the country. Freedom is the highest value of a person's life. Without freedom, a living person does not really have a life. But we must be ready to pay the price for our freedom; i.e. responsible for our decisions and rely on no one to bail us out for any of our bad decisions. Of course, we always thought that we made the right decision at the point of making the said decision. In the hindsight, we must be brave to admit our mistake and have the courage to correct the wrong ourselves. A leader who truly loves his country will aspire to see that all the people are capable of relying on themselves; have faith in the free markets and do no intervention in the everyday life of the people. A leader who makes the people become dependent on the government to look after their welfare is actually the wolf who craves for power and control. Statism disguised as Democratic Socialism (which assumes major and legitimate role in directing the economy and social conducts) is the defunct but most powerful philosophy used by politicians to enslave the people, including the practical men who believe themselves to be quite exempt from any intellectual influence. Associating bad thing with good name often does the trick.

The original Tao Te Jing has only about 5000 words. It was intentional because talking too much about Tao will lead us to deviate from the true Tao. One of the most important philosophies of Lao Zi is that we must not have a fixated mind on what is right and what is wrong. The world is dynamic. The right in a particular time and space may be wrong in another case. Following the same principle, my commentaries and examples quoted (italicized) in relation to various verses of Lao Zi are kept as brief as possible. It is also to avoid making the readers feel bored with too much fringe details that I bring out, especially to those who only wish to know what Lao Zi have said; i.e. the translations. After all, my commentaries are only meant to help the readers understand the unusual ideas of Lao Zi. Interested readers are encouraged to find out the details from the relevant books and the internet. The Chinese texts in this book are the original verses of Lao Zi and are included in the book for easy cross-referencing for readers who understand Chinese language.

Lao Zi and many other ancestors have left a lot of treasures for us. Many who know the Chinese language hold the key to these treasures but they never bother to open the treasure box. Those who do not have the key watch the treasure box with skepticism. What I am doing is to share my discovery with everybody. There are a lot more in the treasure box. Poem translated into another language will inevitably degrade its beauty and value. I am altruistic and selfish at the same time because I hope everybody will become enlightened and the world will become peaceful and safe in which my selfish interest will be served. Diversity is a beauty rather than a problem. The way politicians try to unify and dictate the moral conducts of everybody is too selfish even if they genuinely have a "just cause".

Power, wealth and knowledge must be distributed to the people. When the people are knowledgeable, not only they will be more productive but most importantly they will also be able to do their parts in protecting their country and thus harder for politicians to fool them. The Internet has made a great contribution in this direction. Knowledge is now easily and freely available. I therefore pledge to donate all the proceeds of this publication to non-profit websites such as Ludwig von Mises Institute and Wikipedia to continue their great enthusiasm in spreading useful knowledge which empower the people of the world.

孟子〈万章下〉："伊尹曰：何事非君，何使非民。治亦进，乱亦进，曰：'天之生斯民也，使先知觉后知，使先觉觉后觉。予天民之先觉者也，予将以此道觉此民也。'思天下之民匹夫匹妇有不与被尧舜之泽者，若己推而内之沟中。其自任以天下之重也。"

楚昭王聘孔子，孔子往拜礼焉，路出于陈、蔡。陈、蔡大夫相与谋曰："孔子圣贤，其所刺讥，皆中诸侯之病。若用于楚，则陈、蔡危矣。"遂使徒兵距孔子。孔子不得行，绝粮七日，外无所通，藜羹不充，从者皆病。孔子愈慷慨讲诵，弦歌不衰。乃召子路而问焉，曰："《诗》云：'匪兕匪虎，率彼旷野。'吾道非乎，奚为至于此？"

子路愠，作色而对曰："君子无所困。意者夫子未仁与？人之弗吾信也；意者夫子未智与？人之弗吾行也。且由也，昔者闻诸夫子：'为善者天报之以福，为不善者天报之以祸。'今夫子积德怀义，行之久矣，奚居之穷也？"子曰："由未之识也，吾语汝！汝以仁者为必信也，则伯夷、叔齐不饿死首阳；汝以智者为必用也，则王子比干不见剖心；汝以忠者为必报也，则关龙逢不见刑；汝以谏者为必听也，则伍子胥不见杀。夫遇不遇者，时也；贤不肖者，才也。君子博学深谋而不遇时者，众矣，何独丘哉？且芝兰生于深林，不以无人而不芳；君子修道立德，不谓穷困而改节。为之者，人也；生死者，命也。是以晋重耳之有霸心，生于曹卫；越王勾践之有霸心，生于会稽。故居下而无忧者，则思不远；处身而常逸者，则志不广，庸知其终始乎？"

子路出，召子贡，告如子路。子贡曰："夫子之道至大，故天下莫能容夫子，夫子盍少贬焉？"子曰："赐，良农能稼，不必能穑；良工能巧，不能为顺；君子能修其道，纲而纪之，不必其能容。今不修其道而求其容，赐，尔志不广矣，思不远矣。"

子贡出，颜回入，问亦如之。颜回曰："夫子之道至大，天下莫能容。虽然，夫子推而行之。世不我用，有国者之丑也，夫子何病焉？不容，然后见君子。"孔子欣然叹曰："有是哉，颜氏之子！使尔多财，吾为尔宰。"

Chung Boon Kuan

庄文冠

PART I

TAO [道]

Verse 1

道可道也 非恒道也 名可名也 非恒名也

Tao (or the Great Nature) that is described by anyone will never be the correct or complete description of Tao, because the true Tao is all encompassing and has unlimited extent that it can never be fully described with words. (*Learning from this nature of Tao, we can say that the Way that can be logically explained and convincing to work, is not the Way that will work all the time.*)[1] We may give it a name, but no name can actually befit its greatness. We call it Tao just as a temporary name or a tag. (*Whether it is in science, economics or politics, different theories are developed and given different names, but each theory is only applicable to limited scope of boundary conditions. None of these names can represent the true Tao. This fact suggests that we must not be restricted by rules that human created or religiously follow certain ideology (such as democracy, socialism, Keynesianism, Hayekian, etc.) without questioning its relevance to the dynamics of this complex world. What*

---

[1] The unitalicized sentences are the translations of the prior Chinese texts. The italicised sentences interjected throughout the text are inferences that are not from the original literature.

1

is right may not be always right; what is wrong may not be always wrong; what is good may not be always good; what is bad may not be always bad. For example, being compassionate may be good for developing relationship with each other since interdependency is indispensable but desire for compassion may expose one to the risk of being offered hypocritical compassion and deceived into losing his life, freedom, liberty and property.)

无名 天地之始也 有名 万物之母也

The origin of everything in the universe is nothing, and obviously it has no name as well. Let's call it "Nothingness". Something was started at the beginning of time, we may give it a name called "Existence", and it is the mother of millions of variants. (*There was no rule then, why do we inflict restraint on ourselves? Certain rules may be good to have but they are not without negative implications, and certain rules may be advantageous to one group of people but not for others. Everything has its flip side.*)

故恒无欲 以观其眇也 恒有欲 以观其所徼也

So, we must keep an open mind (*not preoccupied by prior knowledge*) in order to gain insight of the marvelous and far reaching of Tao, but we may need to adopt certain perception (*or certain spectral range of vision, with certain bias or targeted application in mind*) for different scenarios in order to see the form or boundary of certain aspects of Tao. (*For example, everything change with time and space, but there may be certain trend or rhythm that doesn't change. Based on observation, a theory may be developed to explain this behavior, but the theory is not Tao per se.*)

两者同出 异名同谓 玄之又玄 众妙之门

Nothingness and Existence exist together, given different names but they are both part of Tao. (*We have empty space and planets in the universe, both are essential to form the universe. When we look at a cup, we tend to appraise the design but have forgotten that the empty space enclosed by the ceramic body is the one that is actually useful, without which the cup would not be able to hold our favorite coffee and the cup will not be a cup.)* They have convoluted relationship. This is the door to understand the marvelous Tao.

Verse 2
天下皆知美之为美 恶已 皆知善之为善 斯不善矣

When the world adopt a common standard for beautiful, that is ugly. (*For example, in Miss Universe contest, we should not have the perception that skinny girls are beautiful as there are people who view fat girls as beautiful. The winner does not represent the best female in the "Universe" as the judging standard does not take into account the perception of the Martian or other extraterrestrial beings. Having adherence to this fixation we will be biased and see reality as being divided in the preference of certain groups. We must unlearn and relearn constantly to avoid being manipulated or biased in making our choice or decision. In economic theory, the terms such as Gross Domestic Product (GDP) and Consumer Price Index (CPI) are created to fool the people. Politicians would inflate GDP by inflating the bubbles of housing, stocks, or even tulip bulbs. The formula that is used to calculate CPI has been tinkered with over the years such that the artificially manufactured number fits the pre-determined number that the politicians would like to report and fool the people into believing that the politicians were not doing too badly with the economy. We face a huge politica-industria-financia-media machina out there that tries to make us believe things are what they are not.*) When the world adopt a common standard of virtue, it is undesirable. (*There are differences between one value system and another, but we should not like one and dislike the other. "Beautiful" may not be a good attribute, it has its repercussion. Liking beautiful thing is bad, as you may be fooled or tricked by someone who exploits this weakness. Similarly, virtue may not always be good. For example, some governments with their hidden agenda may use the holy name like "human right", or crusade, or other virtuous words, as a cover or an excuse to invade another country and deceive their people to sacrifice in the war. So, being allegiance to a virtuous scheme may expose us to exploitation. Loyalty is "invented" for the advantage of the commanding group while the benefit to the loyalists is actually just the bait. A good leader should care for the well-being of the people, like parents loving their children, and not expect repayment in term of loyalty as he will naturally receive the due respect and support. Leader who likes virtuous individuals may be fooled or tricked by faked personality. Is it better to trust a person who does not need to be forgiven or one who believes that all his sins can be pardoned by simply and privately confessing to his God? Mafia would use virtuous values such as brotherhood love to keep his members together and inflict injustice to non-members. So, the "demand" for virtuous values makes its "supply" valuable, and it can be used as a "tool" for both good and bad intentions. Lie is often wrapped in a noble cause or virtuous excuse. "Fair is foul and foul is fair, hover through the fog and filthy air"—Shakespeare, Macbeth.)*

有无之相生也 难易之相成也 长短之相形也 高下之相盈也 音声之相和也，先后之相随 恒也

Existence and nothingness are opposite but mutually supported. The word difficult existed because there are relatively easier tasks. (*Easier task is not necessarily less meritorious than difficult task.*) We can say certain thing is long because there is comparatively shorter thing. (*Being short is not necessarily disadvantageous compared to long.*) High is relative compared to low, each has its advantage under different circumstances. Sounds of different tones and volume levels are needed to make music. (*Society needs different individuals to do different jobs. It is not a matter of unfairness when some individuals are not born to do certain jobs and stay less prosperous, despite undergoing numerous trainings. It is the work of the Nature and religious beliefs call it fate.*) Front and back depend on which direction is our reference. (*What is in the front is not necessarily more powerful than those at the back. There are events that can only happen after some prior events. We should not feel regret with what that has happened. We should have "the serenity to accept the things that cannot be changed, the courage to change those that can, and the wisdom to know the difference". On the current debt crisis, the European leaders should stop the denials and admit that they have been duped by ill advices of unsound economists and negligent politicians. They must have the courage to make the necessary changes to improve the situation.*) These are all normal occurrences in the Nature. (*The world is beautifully imperfect. Good and bad shall both exist and neither shall be removed from the system. Is poison absolutely bad for health? A little bit of poison may be good to stimulate the body's immune system and becomes resilient against future threat. Is threat (biological, security, financial, etc.) absolutely bad? The existence of threats will make it necessary and rewarding for one to stay alert, ever ready to face challenges, and not complacent with current status. Trying to eliminate all poisons and threats is unwise. "He that struggles with us strengthens our nerves, and sharpens our skill. Our antagonist is our helper."—Edmund Burke*)

是以圣人居无为之事 行不言之教 万物作而弗始也

Hence, great leader only do ordinary, natural, not-ambitious work, and not try to intervene or regulate everything to achieve perfection by somebody's standard. He shall not assume he knows everything and try to teach the people what to do in each and every matter but encourage the people to learn on their own. (*Don't give any advice, especially when one is not requested or there is generation gap. Advice may sometime be construed as a breach of the listener's liberty because he interprets it as a demand for him to comply. It is wrong to impose one's morality on others even if he has a "just cause".*) Everything in this world existed and evolved by themselves and does not require someone to create them one by one. (*The people will be able to find ways to survive without central control or intervention. Let the market sets the necessary standards and regulations. The role of the government is only to defend peoples' lives and properties, by prosecuting fraud and theft, and curb bullying or unfair advantageous, physically and financially. Any law enacted must be for the purpose of protecting the general public who need protection and not for the benefit of rich businessmen to get richer. When Liu Bang toppled the Qin dynasty, he only set three rules for the people to follow. "Step aside and trust in Nature, life will find a way".*)

为而弗恃也 成功而弗居也 夫唯弗居 是以弗去

A good leader does what is necessary to care for the people but doesn't expect anything in return. He will not claim any credit for any success. (*A leader will not be able to get things done single-handedly. A leader can make decision for the country owing to the trust of the people.*) Since he does not need any credit and never aim to earn any credit for whatever he does, he will not worry about losing any credit. (*A leader is expected to act as a role model to motivate the people. A leader should be able to motivate himself and does not need anyone to motivate him, by monetary gain or other means. He is motivated by being able to do what he likes to do or what he lives to believe in. A sportsman strives to win a game for the honor of being a champion. He is rewarded when he earns the title that he deserves. Any additional form of reward is not really needed but a bonus. A country leader takes up the job in order to protect the liberty of the people and himself (rather than letting interventionists and greedy/egoistic/obsessive individuals ruin his beloved country) and be remembered as a good leader; someone whom the people will miss his departure. He is rewarded when he sees the achievements of his leadership. He does not need any other forms of reward. It would be a disgrace to be remembered as a rich politician. Edmund Burke once said: "Applause is the spur of noble minds, the end and aim of weak ones." George Washington presided over the Constitutional Convention that drafted the United States Constitution because he was dissatisfied with the weaknesses of Articles of Confederation in 1787, not because he wanted to be the President of the USA after resigning as commander-in-chief of the Continental Army in the American Revolution. Due to his high prestige, he was unanimously elected the first President in 1789, and again with 100 percent electoral votes in 1792 despite his hesitation to continue the second term.*)

Verse 3
不上贤 使民不争 不贵难得之货 使民不为盗 不见可欲 使民不乱

A leader shall not prefer or give special treatment to clever individuals or pseudo-intellectuals so that the people will not race unnecessarily to be recruited into the government. (*There will always be real intellectuals who shine naturally but not aiming to show off their intelligence to the leader on purpose. It is no good to have ministers who promote themselves into the government for self benefit. When leader shows liking for certain quality, morality or intelligence, he may be fooled by pretenders. For example, when religious quality is highly regarded, people will become fanatical and start to impose unnecessary restrictions on the behavior of everybody, and some people will pretend to be very religious to gain respect and access to the power centers.*) A leader shall not show obsession for rare objects (*like diamond, causing the price to become unnecessarily expensive with unrealistic perceived value*), so that the people will not be lured to commit burglary. (*Herd effects are usually led by influential individuals. Expensive brands of fashions and jewelries are expensive because the idols wear them. There is a flaw in the theory of supply-and-demand of Alfred Marshall because it assumes the market is always rational; clever individuals can use all tactics to change the perception of demand and cause price hike, so much so that even tulip bulbs can fetch a fortune. Similarly, house and stock prices can be propped up by fabricated news flow or artificially cheap loan. In today's world of banking and finance industry, prices of certain commodities are not set by physical demand and physical supply but rather by futures contracts predominantly not backed by physical goods, since there is no intention of physical delivery, which created artificial demand and supply to manipulate the short-term prices. This kind of gambling activities has led to price instability and the collapse of many multinational corporations. Warren Buffett calls it financial weapon-of-mass-destruction.*) A leader shall not portray he is the power center or he has any benefit to be given out, so that the people will not become crazy to get close to him and control him. (*If the government "robs" the people for the politicians and government officers to enjoy lavish lifestyle, some people will feel envy and want to enjoy similar extravagance. They will then endeavor to "steal" the government, or steal from somewhere to satisfy their cravings. If the government is not a power center, no one will want to "steal" the government even if they are paid to do so. Instead, a good leader will safeguard the government machinery by distributing the power to the people so that no one can attempt to turn it into a "personal wealth mining machine".*)

是以圣人之治也 虚其心 实其腹 弱其志 强其骨 恒使民无知无
欲也
使夫知不敢弗为而已 则无不治矣

Great leader governs the society well by not having desire (*for rare objects, luxury food, entertainment, clever individuals, etc.*). His only need is to fill his stomach. He has no big ambition to carry out big project (*such as big building, sophisticated weapon, conquer the world, unify the peoples' mind on what is good and what is bad or religious belief, etc.*). He maintains his health and constantly strengthens his determination to uphold the principles of Tao. He educates the people not to play clever trick and not to be greedy; makes the people know the laws and dare not or don't want to commit a crime, then the society will be peaceful. (*"Men are qualified for civil liberty in exact proportion to their disposition to put moral chains upon their own appetites,—in proportion as their love to justice is above their rapacity,—in proportion as their soundness and sobriety of understanding is above their vanity and presumption,—in proportion as they are more disposed to listen to the counsels of the wise and good, in preference to the flattery of knaves. Society cannot exist, unless a controlling power upon will and appetite be placed somewhere; and the less of it there is within, the more there must be without. It is ordained in the eternal constitution of things, that men of intemperate minds cannot be free. Their passions forge their fetters."—Edmund Burke. If the people think that they cannot live without unlimited entertainment and lavish lifestyle, the mother-earth will not be able to meet their greed. People will start using clever tricks to rob their neighbors and there will be no peace. If the people would rather die or run away from their families instead of working as farmers, there is nothing the mother-earth can help.*)

Verse 4
道冲 而用之有弗盈也 渊兮似万物之宗

Tao is nothingness, so it can accommodate unlimited things and it will never become full. So deep like the source end of everything in the universe. (*Keep an open mind and you will be able to absorb unlimited knowledge, and innovate countless ideas. Steve Jobs once said "lesser artists copy; great artists steal" and "we have always been shameless about stealing great ideas". Few think he was despicable but love what he did instead. Before he dies, he wanted to sue Google and other companies for stealing ideas from Apple Inc. Was he too old or ill to realize that people were merely following his advice? Right and wrong are subjective as far as Tao is concerned. Knowledge belongs to Tao, not to individual who discover it first. If someone wants to keep it secret, like picking up a stone on the earth, he has the right to do so but he has no right to stop others from copying his method and find a similar stone. Unfortunately, we have man-made laws to protect this kind of selfishness to maximize profit to certain companies in the name of encouraging innovation. Companies should instead out-innovate their competitors to maintain their market leadership. By the way, real scientists innovate due to natural interest in science and do not need profiteering laws to motivate them. And, is too much technologies good for us? Are we happier today compared to the past when there was less technologies?)*

挫其锐 解其纷 和其光 同其尘 湛兮 似或存 吾不知其谁之子 象帝之先

Sharp edges become smooth, chaos is resolved, light reflection becomes soft and not sparkling, dust settles into place, the extent is so wide like it has been in this way forever. I don't know who created all these, but it must be the work before the great ancestor. (*Tao is very powerful and able to do all sort of things. It is everywhere and has been around us without our knowledge. Humans did not learn to live together with others in a society yesterday but long ago. We can learn Tao from everywhere. We don't really need to learn from any book or any guru. We are like the fish living in water without knowing the existence or importance of water for it has always been taken for granted. The finger of the guru can point us to the moon but the finger is definitely not the moon. We must raise our head to the sky to appreciate the beauty of the moon ourselves and don't take the words of anyone for granted.*)

Verse 5

天地不仁 以万物为刍狗

The Great Nature has no preferential love. It cares for all things in the universe equally and no selected group receives special care. It treats all things like straw dogs used as offering in sacred ceremony. (*Straw dogs are given careful attention during the ceremony but left alone after that. More rain falls in location A and less in location B is not because the Nature is dearer to the living and non-living things in location A, or the other way around. It rains whenever it wants and not on anyone's request. The Nature has no feeling. It does what it does to nurture all lives and it doesn't care whether it is appreciated or not. It gives what it can afford and doesn't force itself to give more. It cares for everything but doesn't get emotionally attached to anything. It doesn't have a body or form; it is nothingness.*)

圣人不仁 以百姓为刍狗

Great leader shall have no one he especially dears or anyone he disfavors. (*In particular, he does not love the financial-military-industrial complex more than the people.*) He cares for all people equally but at the same time leaves them alone to live and die on their own course. (*A good leader shall not love or give more benefit to someone dearer; no nepotism and no cronyism. A leader shall fulfill his duty in defending the lives and properties of all the people equally; otherwise he would cease to be a leader. But yet, he should only do ordinary, natural, not-ambitious things, and not try to intervene or regulate everything to achieve perfection by somebody's standard. He does what he feels he ought to do and not what others want him to do. Let the people have total freedom to take care of their own lives and do their parts for the country. "The most basic principle to being a free American is the notion that we as individuals are responsible for our own lives and decisions. We do not have the right to rob our neighbors to make up for our mistakes, neither does our neighbor have any right to tell us how to live, so long as we aren't infringing on their rights. Freedom to make bad decisions is inherent in the freedom to make good ones. If we are only free to make good decisions, we are not really free."—Ron Paul*)

天地之间 其犹橐籥乎 虚而不淈 动而愈出 多闻数穷 不若守于中

The space between the sky and the earth is like a bellow pipe. It is empty but it doesn't warp. The more it moves the more wind and sound it produces. It is never exhausted. But too much of it will create trouble. It is best to be moderate. (*A good leader would provide any possible assistance to the people especially when there is a natural disaster. In other times, he will provide assistance when he thinks he ought to, is able, willing and ready to do it. He shall exercise moderation. He may help the people but not too much. He will not make the country a welfare state. Maintaining wealth equality shall not be turned into nationalized charity. The people must rely on themselves rather than the government. This is the foundation of personal liberty. Nobody is coerced to make more contribution in order to subsidize certain groups. One cannot expect to have freedom while at the same time expect to be cradled and disciplined like a child. Too much welfare is no welfare because it becomes entitlement and decays the people abilities to rely on themselves. At the end, the politicians will have to "Rob Peter to pay Paul" in order to maintain their heroic cover and gain the people's votes. When the country goes bankrupt, "the phoenix will have to be burned into ashes before it can be reborn". We must be careful with what we ask for from the government. There is no free lunch. Free medical care gives the people false sense of security and misleads them into neglecting their health until it is too late to find out that even modern medical science is no magical spell. Medical care is a poor substitute for health care which is associated with hygiene, proper diet, exercise, and lifestyle. Ultimately, who pays the bill? Who gets the biggest slice of the allocation? Could it be pharmaceutical companies, health care industries, insurance corporations, bankers, and politicians? As Ludwig von Mises puts it, the state is just a legalized force, and its only function is to defend lives and properties of the people by beating antisocial elements into submission. As for the rest, government is "the employment of armed men, of policemen, gendarmes, soldiers, prison guards, and hangmen. The essential feature of government is the enforcement of its decrees by beating, killing, and imprisonment. Those who are asking for more government interference are asking ultimately for more compulsion and less freedom." A deer would choose to live in the wild if it wants freedom. If it wishes to be looked after, it will have to*

11

live in a cage. No two ways about it. The Medicare and Medicaid schemes in the US have become underfunded due to overconsumption of hospitals, escalating medical cost and impact of demographic change on annual collection of the funds. The government is forced to pay the demand of medical care contractors so that they will not agitate the patients covered by the schemes into venting dissatisfaction and frustration onto the government. Knowing the government will always pay, pharmaceutical companies and doctors will increase charges with excuses of rising costs and "mandatory" immunizations, justified by ever innovatively fabricated facts, and they will always get their way. In the end, it is not in the best interest of the people and the government. The people are forced to foot increasing prices of medical care and the government is blackmailed into paying the contractors.)

(Paul Krugman, Economics Nobel laureate, wrote in a textbook Macroeconomics (2nd ed., published in 2009): "Public policy designed to help workers who lose their jobs can lead to structural unemployment as an unintended side effect . . . . In other countries, particularly in Europe, benefits are more generous and last longer. The drawback to this generosity is that it reduces a worker's incentive to quickly find a new job. Generous unemployment benefits in some European countries are widely believed to be one of the main causes of 'Eurosclerosis,' the persistent high unemployment that affects a number of European countries." Anyway, the former Enron adviser flip-flopped over his stand in 2010 and said "giving money to the unemployed is a very fast, effective way of creating jobs". To listen or not to listen to economist, that is the question. If "lack of demand for the things workers produce" is limiting employment, then giving money for the unemployed to spend is just a short-term economic life support and it is not sustainable because the money will most likely be used to pay imported low-cost groceries rather than costly locally produced goods and services. How many jobs, that match the skill-set of the unemployed, can be created? If lobster is no longer in demand, it doesn't make economic sense to continue supporting the lobstermen and the unviable business using government subsidy. Unemployment is not a "social evil" but a signal for changes to be made. Re-adjustment of the free-market system can be disrupted if false impression that "politicians can possibly help the unemployed" is given. Everybody must realize that the market

is cold-hearted (even more so the politicians, who are only kind-hearted to their cronies and pretending to be angels to poor people) so that no one becomes dull to the risk of continuing unviable businesses and refuse to re-adjust when the needs arise. Out of self-interest, entrepreneurs will be out attempting to create new jobs for unemployed men and serve the interest of the nation, by the way. Real wages will increase with greater production, if the products really have a market and not some useless or uncompetitive toys or non-essential financial gambling packages. However, these will be prevented from happening when the Minimum Wage law (set wages higher than the actual minimum amount for one to avoid starvation) and other employee benefit laws (extended maternity leave, for example) make businesses not economically viable, forcing entrepreneurs to be more entrepreneurial and taking their businesses elsewhere or outsourcing it. The true evil behind unemployment problem, apart from unemployment compensation and Minimum Wage Law, is wastage of fund on big government which is not productive but sucks away the fund required for healthy operation of the free-market. To this end, the tax payers shall have no obligation to pay more bureaucrats and government servants for counter-productive works they did; no mercy in response to their misbehaviors and bureaucracies.)

Verse 6
浴神不死 是谓玄牝 玄牝之门 是谓天地之根 绵绵呵 其若存 川之不堇

The energy source which created the universe will not die off. It is the mysterious womb which created everything in the universe. The door to this mysterious womb is the root of the sky and earth; so soft and enormous. It seems to exist but not visible. It can be used forever and will never be exhausted.

Verse 7
天长 地久 天地之所以能长且久者 以其不自生也 故能长生

The sky and earth have existed for so long. Why they are so long lasting is because they don't selfishly live their own life but share with everything in

13

the natural world. The symbiosis gave them the longevity. (*A king cannot live alone but can only survive if the people live and give him the necessary moral and material support. God cannot survive if there is no worshiper. Believers are the makers of God. People will one day realize that they need to do good not because God or some written rules tell them to but for their own survival in this world. Humans are social animals that depend on each other and can only live on mutual co-operation to defend themselves against "tigers", "clever thieves" and other threats. They don't need to be given the promise of entrance ticket to heaven when the purpose of doing-good is well understood and the people are intelligent enough to embrace it as a natural thing to do. The basic of doing-good is doing no harm to anyone. Doing-good is the only way to maintain harmony for mutual self-interest. Doing-good need not have to be motivated by a foreseeable reciprocation or reward because one is already rewarded with the benefit of being able to live in a harmonious society. Receiving special good deed from someone is a bonus.*)

是以圣人后其身而身先 外其身而身存 不以其无私邪 故能成其私

Great leader puts behind his head about where he will stand to gain something. He will then be supported and given the top leadership role. He shall not worry about his safety and he will be protected and survive. (*All the great leaders in history were remembered because they were selfless, not calculative on their personal risk or benefit, they didn't feel any risk they took was unbearable, they did what they thought they ought to do and that gave them the strength to persevere, and they survived and cherished. They thought of themselves less but, at the end, they gained much from their endeavors. Genuine selflessness is not thinking less of yourself, but thinking of yourself less. If you are the rightful leader that the people want you to lead, they will protect you and will not let anything bad happen to you. The people will worry about your safety more than you do. Leader who craves for loyalty is not a good leader. After victory over Great Britain in the American Revolutionary War as commander-in-chief of the Continental Army, George Washington resigned rather than seize power, proving his opposition to dictatorship. He was subsequently made by unanimous choice to serve as the first President of the USA.*) Because he is not selfish, his self-interest is fulfilled by being able to live in a peaceful country, and granted with the benefit to be at the top. (*Everyone, including the leader, have genuine self-interest in the well-being of the country. It is a luxury to be able to live in a peaceful country and enjoy personal liberty. Economy malaise, wealth inequalities, and social injustice can lead to destruction of a country, as demonstrated by the recent uprisings in Arab countries and numerous examples in the world's history.*)

Verse 8

上善若水 水善利万物而不争 居众人之所恶 故几于道矣

The best quality has the characteristic of the water. Water provides benefits to all things but never compete with them for anything, and it absorbs everything that others discard. This characteristic is close to Tao. (*Give all benefits to the people, and be accommodative for any grouses or dissatisfactions since these are expected because perfection was never intended and it's impossible to please everybody. The people are the "shareholders" or "bosses" of the country, while the government is the "management team" hired by the people. When the government is not performing as expected, it has to be mentally ready to endure the scolding of the "bosses", not the other way around. Muammar Gaddafi and other dictators were dead wrong to assume they are above the people. It is ridiculous to expect the "bosses" to obey the "employees" as opposed to obeying the wishes of the majority "shareholders". "All human laws are, properly speaking, only declaratory; they have no power over the substance of original justice." —Edmund Burke*)

居善地 心善渊 予善仁 言善信 正善治 事善能 动善时 夫唯不争 故无尤

A leader may learn from the water. He shall be wise in taking his position (*as the servant of the people*), keep his heart accommodative, generous in giving, truthful with his words, uphold righteous in his ruling to prosecute crimes, work effectively, and do the right thing at the right timing. Because he does not compete with the people, therefore no one would hate him.

(The government has no business to be in business. Business shall be left to the people. The government should only do what it could to facilitate the business growth and leave the benefits to the people. When the people are rich, the government can never be poor. The leader should be generous in helping needy people as much as he could, but not without caution of deviating from the principle of Tao. Using public fund to do charity is robbing all the people to give it to selected groups. It would be best for the public to set up charitable funds rather than going through the bureaucracy of the government. Some politicians like to privatize debt and nationalize charity to buy votes. We must be careful with this trick. It is more prudent to emphasize men relating to each other voluntarily to get any assistance they need. The Nature is cold-hearted, but it survives through symbiosis with everything in the world. The free-market is cold-hearted, but it survives through interdependence among one another. The government must avoid becoming a benevolent nanny. Any programs funded by tax payers' money (such as education, youth development, public health, sports, family aids, defense, etc.) should not be motivated by compassion but aim at attaining the overall health of the social and economic systems; i.e. social justice, wealth equality, economic growth, and national security. As such, the effectiveness of the programs shall be measured in these key performance areas. For example, are the school leavers more productive? Are the youth more responsible for themselves and the society? Is the public health budget decreasing due to better knowledge of personal health information, hygienic practices, and healthier lifestyle? Are families more harmonious and single-families more self-reliant, giving less social problems and street crimes? Is the government making more friends rather than enemies? Are national treats removed rather than requiring more defense budget to acquire high-tech junks that make everybody suffer just to catch a few criminals? The logical conclusions of ethical self-interest and concern for others are actually the same. Selfishness and altruism can be opposite and yet parallel.)

Verse 9

殖而盈之 不如其已 揣而锐之 不可长葆也 金玉盈室 莫之能守
也 富贵而骄 自遗咎也 功遂身退 天之道也

Don't accumulate too many trophies until the room is full but stop at the right timing. A blade sharpened too much will not last long. Fill a house with gold and jade and no one will be able to protect it. Being wealthy and proud is asking for trouble. A leader should retire after he has accomplished his task. This is the way of the Great Nature. (*Some leaders do not know when to stop. They keep sharpening their skills, thinking that they can continue to do what they are good at and will never fail forever. Look at Alexander the Great and Genghis Khan. Some leaders accumulate all the wealth thinking that they can keep them forever. Some assume they have great power and they can abuse anyone as they like. Look at the kingdoms that were toppled by the people. Becoming rich while most people are in poverty will make wealth turning into a curse rather than a blessing. Many people will eye for any opportunity to take possession of the wealth. The natural resources in Africa have been a curse because they have become something for the strongest thugs to steal. The governments of these countries have become prizes sought after by various tribes, to be exclusively used as vehicles for theft and repression, for profit and to reward buddies. Keeping all the money in a safe deposit box makes it easy for a thief to take them all. Distributing it will make sure no one thief can take all. The same applies to centralized power. Power, wealth and knowledge must be distributed to the people. When the people are knowledgeable, not only they will be more productive but most importantly they will also be able to do their parts in protecting their country and it is harder for politicians to fool them.*)

Verse 10

戴营魄抱一 能毋离乎
榑气致柔 能婴儿乎
修除玄监 能无疵乎

The soul and the body are together. Can they stay that way and not separated forever?

Breathing in more air can make the body soft. Can it make the body as soft as a baby?

Purify the mind and carry out deep reflection. Can there be no imperfection at all? (*Do what we can and don't be idealistic. We will surely make a few bad decisions along with good ones. Perfectionism will lead to extremism. Try to follow any scientific health advices but accept the fact that there is no guarantee of a life free of cancer or other illnesses. One of the teachings of Buddhism tells us that life is naturally full of sufferings or unpleasant events. If we accept this fact, we shall not feel too depressed when we face multiple misfortunes because that is normal, the nature of life, and no one can escape from this fate at one period or another in the journey to death. Happiness and sadness are within us, not in the surroundings. It is up to us to let our feeling be affected by the surrounding events.*)

爱民治国 能毋以知乎
天门启阖 能为雌乎
明白四达 能毋以知乎

In loving the people and governing the country, is it possible to achieve a state where intelligence need not be applied? (*This is indeed idealistic which is only possible when the country is so peaceful and the people live happily and need nothing from the government. The leader needs not and should not do anything to disturb the status quo. But no system can work without the right people to operate it. We must not fantasize having a perfect system that runs itself even if the leader is an idiot. Ideally, the leader should not favor one group of people over another. In practice, for the sake of correcting wealth inequality, the government may need to do some "necessary evils" such as being "Robin Hood" in taxing the rich to subsidize the poor. But he must do it intelligently so that this kind of social welfare needs not be too much for too long. The danger of a leader being opportunistic or using clever tricks is it will serve as a model in educating the people to use similar tactics against other people or even against the government.*) When the body senses interact with the surrounding, is it possible to show no agitation and stay serene like the female? (*Even if there are some problems that arise from time to time, the leader should not take drastic action. Stay calm at all times.*) In studying and understanding everything around us, can we not aim to use those knowledge ever? (*Shouldn't we learn martial arts but hope we never have to use it? Shouldn't we learn lifesaving skills but hope we never have to be a hero? Opportunity, including opportunity to save ourselves, is reserved for individuals who are prepared. Learn anything and everything without calculating their usefulness. Great leaders do not become great by just studying the traits of past leaders. They learnt everything along their journey of life and did not think that they ever need to use those knowledge. Sometimes, they are not even aware that they have used some of the knowledge they learnt ages ago. No businessman can become successful by fantasizing they can become successful just by reading a few books on business, management, leadership, or have a mentor. Our footprint is no greater than one square foot but it doesn't mean we don't need more land to stand on. The "useless" soil supported the soil that we stand on. We don't use all the knowledge we learnt in school but it doesn't mean those not used are useless because they have reinforced the knowledge that we do use. Education is about the process of improving brain power, permanent change of behavior, and not merely about how much knowledge is accumulated at the end. Everything we study contributes to improving our brain power. Furthermore, the knowledge not used now may be needed in the future. The great carpenter cannot teach his son how to become a great carpenter. He can teach his son the required skills but he cannot possibly pass on the art. The son will never become a great carpenter if he only practices carpentry and has no appreciation for art and the beauty of Nature. Steve Jobs once said: "I decided to take a calligraphy class to learn how to do calligraphy.*

I learnt about serif and sans-serif typefaces, about varying the space between different letter combinations, about what makes great typography great. It was beautiful. Historical. Artistically subtle in a way that science can't capture. And I found it fascinating. None of this had any hope of any practical application in my life. But 10 years later, when we were designing the first Macintosh computer, it all came back to me. And we designed it all into the Mac. It was the first computer with beautiful typography. If I had never dropped in on that single course in college, the Mac would never have multiple typefaces or proportionally spaced fonts. And since Windows just copied the Mac, it's likely that no personal computer would have them.")

生之 畜之 生而弗有 长而弗宰 是谓玄德

Tao created all things and nurture them, but it doesn't own or possess them. It raises them but not controlling them. (*Some political leaders assume that their "just cause" give them the rights, even the responsibility, to impose their morality or value system on the people in order to achieve their personal political objectives. Some mother-in-laws do the same thing. It is so wrong to force people to want something that they don't really want. It doesn't make it right even if it is done by democratic means. "Individual rights are not subject to a public vote; a majority has no right to vote away the rights of a minority; the political function of rights is precisely to protect minorities from oppression by majorities."—Ayn Rand*) This kindness is called the Great Benevolence.

Verse 11
卅辐同一毂 当其无 有车之用也
埏埴而为器 当其无 埴器之用也
凿户牖 当其无 有室之用也
故 有之以为利 无之以为用

30 spokes around the center of a wheel share one hub. Because the hub has an empty space at the center, therefore it can accommodate an axle for a car to move over the ground. Cup can be made from clay hardened by

heat. Because it has an empty space in the middle, therefore it can function as a container. In making a house, the empty space in the middle makes it useful as a house. (*We shall never overlook the usefulness of emptiness or take it for granted. If we fill it up with too many things, it will lose its function.*) So, the solid part provides the convenience of handling or defining the object, the empty part provides the usefulness. (*In governing a country, laws and procedures may be necessary for common people or officers to easily follow and produce consistent but mediocre results, but let us not forget the ultimate purpose of the laws and procedures when they were yet to be drafted, i.e. to create orderly society for the common benefit of the people. We must always revisit this purpose or spirit rather than insisting on following the procedures. Procedures are non-living things, not the God that we must submit to, and what is important is the outcome. Insisting on 100% compliance of the procedures often let loose the criminals who exploit the legal procedures. So, the legal procedures must not be too detailed or complex.*)

Verse 12

五色使人之门盲 五音使人之耳聋 五味使人之口爽 驰骋畋猎使人心发狂 难得之货使人之行方 是以圣人之治也 为腹而不为门 故去彼而取此

Obsession for everything to be colorful makes people blind. (*Blind in the sense that he cannot find value in plain non-colorful things. Blind in the sense that he brushes aside wise individuals who do not have a smooth look.*) Obsession for music makes people deaf. (*Deaf in the sense that he only want to hear what he wants to hear and disregard wise but bitter advices.*) Obsession for taste makes people lose his appetite for healthy natural foods. (*A person may develop eating disorder to the detriment of his physical and mental health. Obsession for taste of success or achievement makes one forgets the wonderful taste of graceful family life.*) Horse racing and animal hunting make people go mad and foolish. (*A person with unsettling mind will not be able to make rational reasoning or enjoy serene living, calm and do nothing extraordinary.*) Obsession for rare objects or jewelries makes people lose their personal conduct. (*A person who relies on jewelry to gain self confidence will always feel not confident when he compares himself with other people. Similarly, a person who values a specific skill or knowledge too much will feel shy or have low self-esteem when there is a real expert in the room.)* Therefore, great leader will only desire to fill his stomach and has no obsession for any valuable stuff and entertainment. He practices serenity so that he is not contaminated by the abovementioned undesirable traits.

Verse 13
宠辱若惊 贵大患若身

A leader should feel alarm over honor similar to that over insult. He should take priority on national disaster like it is happening to his body.

何谓宠辱若惊 宠之为下也 得之若惊 失之若惊 是谓宠辱若惊

Why should he feel alarm over honor similar to that over insult? A person can be honored only if he is inferior to someone or something (*such as the Institution of the People*). When he is honored, he should feel alarm because the honor comes with expectation and burden to keep that honor. (*It may not be wise to do too much and strive for glory. "Students of social science must fear popular approval: Evil is with them when all men speak well of them."—Alfred Marshall*) He will feel alarm if he loses the honor. (*He can lose the honor especially when he forgets to be humble and starts behaving arrogantly.*) Therefore, he should feel alarm over honor similar to that over insult.

何谓贵大患若身 吾所以有大患者 为吾有身 及吾无身 有何患

Why should he take priority on national disaster like it is happening to his body? Disaster can have effect on me because I have a body. If I don't have a body, I will have no worry over disaster. (*Everyone has a genuine self-interest in the security, economy, wealth equality and social justice of his country. Threat to the system affects everybody, including the leader. This makes it the busi-ness of everyone to be busy-body about it. It is in the selfish best-interest of anyone that motivated seemingly selfless actions to safeguard this Greater Self. If you are not a resident of Somalia, you will have no worries over what happen in Somalia. While we are in our home, chaos happening in our country will affect all of us. We hope we never have to be someone like Sun Yat Sen because we hope we never get into such dire situation to need a hero. Even if we are humble citizens and don't endeavor to become someone like Sun Yat Sen, we must at least do our very least by giving our support to someone who tries to prevent the country from drifting towards perdition. Never underestimate your worth, never be afraid to face the coercion from the bully when you have to, and have the dignity to reject pretentious generosity and filthy lucre bait to fish your vote. We must not allow bullying to become a rewarding thing to do and it will be too late when a cruel regime is formed. Bankruptcy of the country is the last thing we want to endure in our life. Whatever you plan for your children will become meaningless if the desired environment is destroyed before they even grow up.)*

故贵为身以为天下 若可托天下 爱己身以为天下 女可以寄天下

Therefore, a leader should be one who accentuates self-reliance and personal liberty and wish to extend it to all people in the country. (*He doesn't need any praise or honor. So, he will educate the people not to expect generosity from him or the government, neither will he "rob" the people with taxation and repression, both in terms of finance and morality. On the other hand, he is mindful that he is part of the society. For his selfish best-interest, he will do the necessary to safeguard the health of the society in terms of security, economy, wealth equality and social justice. Self-interest is not an evil. It is the motivation for anyone to take good care of himself and the environment he lives in. Ethical self-interest should be promoted. Ethics itself is motivated by long-term self-interest. Win-win is the keyword for long-term trust. Altruism of the church is sustained by self-interest in the form of promise of an entrance ticket to the heaven. Patriotism is unreliable. Of course, for many great leaders in history, self-interest is in the subconscious and they don't calculate it everyday, as advocated in Verse 7, but their self-interest is eventually served by the "Invisible Hand". Priests, poets, or politicians can sometimes harangue others to do things for love or charity. However, self-interest of the people will be far more reliable, effective, and efficient to motivate and coordinate voluntary cooperation on a large scale to serve the needs of others. When we want to promote something, we must tell the customers what they stand to gain. For example, people will love others when they are reminded that they will be loved. Haranguing the people to do something for patriotism sake will not work most of the time, unless the people are naïve. We are already patriotic when we are not a liability to society. No country can prosper if the self-interest of individual citizen is not safeguarded. Individuals who are truly selfless are pitiful because they have no self which means they have no life but just some machines programmed to serve the needs of others. And their ability to exit the inherent program code execution loop is disabled such that they will always think that they are conscious, because they do feel happy as a reward to be of service to others, no matter how hard someone tries to wake them up. The "Rise of the Machines" must be prevented. We have seen many youngsters being turned into "machines" which carry bombs and explode themselves in public places in the name of holy war. We have also seen many Christian followers being turned into "machines" to serve selflessly in warzone in the name of humanitarian causes. On the other hand, individuals who are unethically selfish are also machines programmed to want something. It can be difficult to educate them to change their behavior permanently or make them see the reality that human beings are social animals that cannot survive alone like a tiger could by nature but require cooperation to defend themselves for common interest. Mutual trust is the prerequisite for cooperation to be effective. Possessing the power to do something feels so good. This is natural in humans as well as in animals. Many individuals like to do random acts of kindness with no expectation of any return. The fact that they are able to do good to someone or to Mother-earth gives them a burst of endorphins. It serves as an incentive to do good, motivates self-interest in the subconscious, on top of the belief that what goes around comes around. This is another example of altruism and ethical self-interest come to the same logical conclusion. Individuals who are not able to do good will not be able to understand the good feeling of those endorphins.)* He can then be entrusted with the leadership of the country. He shall be one who loves individual rights and freedom above everything else and wishes to extend it to all people. (*He will look after the country like looking after himself because it concerns his rights and freedom.*) The country can then be entrusted to his care. (*A person who is honest about doing good for self-interest and respect the self-interest of the people can then be trusted as opposed to a person who pretends to be selflessly noble. A person who loves glory more than his life will not care for the lives of others. He will not hesitate to provoke war, play on the patriotism of the people to mislead them into a belief in the great fallacy of war, and drag the people into war. A person who claims he loves his country and everyone else more than himself is a liar. He must have a selfish agenda behind his pretended "selfless" when in actual fact he is just greedy/egoistic/obsessive although he may be genuinely patriotic; he has no right to shape or color the country according to his personal whims and fancies without the approval of the people. Look at the leaders of revolutions in history. They started to join the revolts because they were fighting for their own liberty, not because they love the people more than themselves. The leaders who finally succeeded were those who cared for the people, therefore commanded the support of the people, and they were merely leading the people who fought for liberty which was the common goal of the people and the leader. No one would sacrifice for the sole benefit of the leader; unless he is blackmailed or brainwashed by the leader. Some parents may be selfless to sacrifice their lives in protecting their children in emergency situation. This is a different story and it is natural.*)

Verse 14

视之而弗见 名之曰微 听之而弗闻 名之曰希 捪之而弗得 名之曰夷 三者不可致诘
故混而为一

Tao cannot be seen, cannot be heard, and cannot be touched. Because of these three properties, it cannot be thoroughly investigated. Therefore, we can only lump together and called it Tao.

一者 其上不谬 其下不惚 寻寻呵 不可名也 复归于无物 是谓无
状之状 无物之象
是谓沕望 随而不见其后 迎而不见其首 执今之道 以御今之有
以知古始 是谓道纪

It is one-piece, where there is no discontinuity above and below it. It is infinite and cannot be named (*because it has no boundary to be identified and differentiated from something else*). It finally converges to nothingness. It has the shape of no shape, the appearance of nothingness. Following behind it could not see its back. Facing it could not see its head. (*We can neither analyze the effect of Tao as it is happening nor retrospectively. There was a time when America looked down on Japan for the latter's inability to deal with its economic stagnation problems. Just as the Americans thought that they have identified the misstep of Japan, the purported miracle cure of Quantitative Easing is not working. America is now realizing how difficult a post bubble economy can be when the root cause is not tackled.*) We can try to hold on to what we know about Tao today (*i.e. all the Laws and Theories developed*) to deal with the phenomena around us, extrapolate it to figure out the origin, and generalize the trend or cycle. (*This is a method used by physicists in the study of the physical world and the universe.*)

Verse 15
古之善为道者 微眇玄达 深不可志
夫唯不可志 故强为之容 曰 与呵 其若冬涉水 犹呵 其若畏四邻
俨呵 其若客 涣呵
其若冰泽 沌呵 其若朴 湷呵 其若浊 旷呵 其若谷

There were practitioners of Tao in the past. They had fine knowledge and wisdom. Their behavioral traits have deep implications and cannot be described in words. Because they cannot be described, some subjective depictions are: they were careful in their actions as if they were crossing frozen river during winter; they were cautious as if they were fearful of any ill intention of the surrounding neighbors; they were courteous as if they were a guest; they were warm hearted like ice melting during the spring; they had pure feelings toward all (*no faked expression of cheer or grief*), like natural material that are untouched; what's in their mind was not deducible, like murky water; they were accommodative, like the valley. (*A leader should be gentle like a deer, but not as defenseless as deer: careful in his action, cautious of any danger, not confrontational, generous, sincere, reserve in expressing opinions, forgiving and accept different opinions. George Washington was careful in all his actions because he was aware that everything he did set a precedent; avoided war with Great Britain by securing the Jay Treaty in 1795; stayed neutral in foreign wars; brought rival factions together to unify the nation; paid off all states and national debt; solicitous of the opinion of others; talked regularly with department heads and listened to their advice before making a final decision; forgave Secretary of the State Thomas Jefferson who went against him and did not dismiss Jefferson from his cabinet.*)

浊而静之徐清　安以动之　徐生　保此道者不欲盈　夫唯不欲盈　故能蔽而不成

Murky water left to settle down will slowly become clear. Quiet state being stirred will slowly become active. (*Life is repeated cycles from passive state to active and then back to passive again, but it would be best for the changes to take place slowly and gracefully.*) Practitioners of Tao followed this natural cycle and never wanted to carry too far. Because they never wanted to carry too far, therefore they never become perfect. (*The universe is beautifully imperfect and it should be left naturally that way rather than artificial perfection. Perfectionism is bad. Wanting to achieve perfection will be stressful and unwise. Achieving perfection means it is time to start decaying. Being imperfect means there is room for improvement. This is one of the spirits of Yi Jing. The boom and bust of economic cycle are inevitable. It is not a myth but a phenomenon that can be scientifically explained. Intervention to prolong the boom will make the eventual bust more painful. It is best to let the economic cycle takes its natural course of corrections from time to time and the peaks and valley will be of lesser magnitude. The cycle of joy and sorrow in life is also inevitable. It is not quantifiable and does not follow any simple periodic pattern but it is the proven fact of life. We should not seek too much joy or use stimulant because more sorrow will follow and the long-term trend may be downward rather than upward. It is best to practice self-restrain on our needs and wants. The cycle of four seasons is natural. Trying to stop the arrival or departure of the spring season is stupid.* 蠢)

Verse 16

致虚 极也 守静 笃也 万物旁作 吾以观其复也
天物芸芸 各复归于其根 曰静 静 是谓复命
复命 常也 知常 明也 不知常 妄 妄作 凶

Becoming serene is the final destination. Stay tranquil is to be practiced persistently. All things live together in this world differently. I can observe they all go through cycle of life and death. There are so many different life forms. All of them will eventually return to their original state, i.e. the state of tranquility. Tranquility is the revolving end of life cycle. Cycle of life is a natural rule that never change. Accepting the natural rule is wise. Refuse to accept the natural rule is arrogant. Arrogant undertaking will lead to bad consequences. (*We all come to this world with nothing, and we will be back to nothing when we die. Why should we be too ambitious for success and prosperity? Why and to whom we need to prove our worth? Are we not fooled by some unnecessary value system created by someone? We can work hard and accumulate resources to prepare for rainy days. But it is not wise to work for the sake of glory and regret later for not having a life. Great power and wealth come with great responsibility. Obsession for success is destined to face a string of failures along the way. This is the sub-cycle of life; No pain no gain, more gain more pain. Since we come to this world with nothing, we will surely gain something when we die. But 100% of our capital gain will be taxed by the government or somebody else.*)

知常 容 容乃公 公乃王 王乃天 天乃道 道乃久 殁身不殆

Accepting the natural rule of life cycle will bring about tolerance. Tolerance will bring about fairness. Fairness leads to appropriate decision and action. Appropriateness leads to natural righteous. Righteous leads to Tao. Upholding Tao brings about durability, and allow one to avoid peril for the whole life. (*Knowing that we will die some day should make us more tolerant of other's doing and not too calculative on gain and loss. Subsequently, we will want to be fair to others. When we are fair and not selfish, we will be able to make correct decision that is for common good. Therefore, it is truly righteous and not just righteous according to somebody's standard. And because it is naturally right, it is close to Tao. If we master the fundamental principle of Tao, we can apply it to solve various problems of different backgrounds; thus, not requiring long list of laws and rules, each for addressing limited scope of problems. Based on Tao, we will be able to take appropriate actions to solve any problems we face throughout our journey to the end of our natural life. Rules and procedures are drafted by leaders for officers and operators to easily follow and produce consistent but mediocre results. A bureaucrat is 'an official who is rigidly devoted to the details of administrative procedure.' Bureaucrats are not expected to be thinkers, innovators, or men of action. A good leader should not rely on rules and procedures in decision making if he wishes to obtain excellent results.*)

Here are a few quotes from Steve Jobs about death:

- *I have looked in the mirror every morning and asked myself: "If today were the last day of my life, would I want to do what I am about to do today?" And whenever the answer has been "No" for too many days in a row, I know I need to change something.*
- *Death is the destination we all share, no one has ever escaped it. And that is as it should be because death is very likely the single best invention of life.*
- *Your time is limited, so don't waste it living someone else's life. Don't be trapped by dogma—which is living with the results of other people's thinking. Don't let the noise of others' opinions drown out your own inner voice. And most important, have the courage to follow your heart and intuition. They somehow already know what you truly want to become. Everything else is secondary.*

- *Remembering that I'll be dead soon is the most important tool I've ever encountered to help me make the big choices in life. Because almost everything—all external expectations, all pride, all fear of embarrassment or failure—these things just fall away in the face of death, leaving only what is truly important. Remembering that you are going to die is the best way I know to avoid the trap of thinking you have something to lose. You are already naked. There is no reason not to follow your heart.*

- *No one wants to die. Even people who wanna go to heaven don't wanna die to get there.*

Verse 17

太上 下知有之 其次 亲誉之 其次 畏之 其下 侮之

The best government is one that the people know it existed but doesn't feel its interference (*minimum tax, minimum regulation, and minimum welfare*). The second best government is one that the people love and praise it. The third is government that the people fear it. And the worst is government that the people hate and despise. (*People in democratic countries are made to believe that "they somehow have a stake in the government, they are the government." But the fact is: if the government overwhelms the people it supposed to protect with its monopoly of force, the people must obey whatever the government said (including taking away their properties in the name of saving the economy, intrusion of their privacies in the name of national security, shutting their mouths with alleged sedition in the name of maintaining social order, etc.), the people don't really have a stake in the government. Whenever there are power centers, some people will attempt to capture and gain control of the power centers. No good leader would want to be a puppet, and no good people would want their country to be dominated by "financiers". For the common benefit of the country, the power of the government must be limited, so much so that the people can carry on their daily lives with little interference from the government, benevolent or otherwise. When the government has little money to spend, greedy individual will not want to be in the government, bankers and business corporations will leave the government alone, except*

30

that they can still influence the government to make regulations that are advantageous to them but seemingly benefit the people. The people must say no to this kind of "benevolence". If the voters can be bought, directly or indirectly, it is not a true democratic system. It is just a regime hiding behind the facade of democratic politics. Democracy cannot be good for the country if the people keep voting "movie stars" into the government because most people do not have the sophistication to identify the right leader based on the appearance but instead fooled by the most charming and sweet talking candidate.)

信不足 案有不信 猷呵 其贵言也 功成事遂 而百姓皆谓我自然

If the government is not trustworthy, it will not be trusted by the people. (*He who is not trustworthy will usually call for the people to "trust in God" as if he is God sent and "he trust in God, therefore the people must trust him", but in truth he is just craving for self-interest. Muammar Gaddafi of Libya is one example, so are the numerous examples in the world's history. A trustworthy leader will not need to make use of God to back him up. Instead, he uses his action and inaction to gain the people's trust.*) The government must think twice before making any proclamation or regulation. (*Instead, the government should work on projects, such as public infrastructure, canal, dam, open up farmland, etc. that will facilitate the success of the people in producing goods.*) When success is achieved and all endeavors went well, the people can claim they achieve the success themselves as they never feel they ever receive any substantial help from the government. (*Empower the people instead of setting stumbling blocks with unnecessary regulations. Help the people along the way but let them be responsible for their lives and decisions. Give all the credits to the people. The father of Yu was executed because he failed to resolve the flooding problem of River Huang despite the huge budget and support from Emperor Shun and the people. Yu was then entrusted to correct the works of his father and led the people in building canals and levees. Upon the death of Emperor Shun, Yu was made the successor due to his achievement in resolving the Great Flood. Emperor Yu then started the Xia dynasty. For decades, people were able to obtain great harvest and free of flood disaster, and the people never felt it was the benevolence of Yu anymore.*

Instead, they felt everything was given by the Nature and their own hard work. Emperor Yu was pleased to know that. Unfortunately, the convention of meritorious succession was broken after his death, albeit not by his will, and succession by birth ensued.)

Verse 18

故大道废 案有仁义 知慧出 案有大伪 六亲不和 案有孝慈 邦家昏乱 案有贞臣

When the society is in chaos, it is the circumstance that villains will use compassion and morality (*due to the lack of "supply" and therefore the "price" goes up*) to attract followers or as ground for extenuating their crime. (*A gangster head may use fairness in distributing robbery gain to assemble the members. Or he may declare he will only rob the rich and give charity to the poor.*) When brilliance becomes most enviable, big frauds will become widespread. (*Brilliant Wall-Street's executives invented various squalid ways to steal massive wealth for themselves and used the White House revolving door to get away with their frauds. The various empires invented various "virtuous reasons" to colonize or steal someone's country and yet feel proud to record in their history books and show no sign of repentance. Stealing is punishable under the laws but yet the museums in the United Kingdom are proud to show the relics they stole from China and other parts of the world. The younger generations can now ask why they cannot steal while their ancestors and current leaders felt proud of doing it in the past. What a good educational example.*) When family members are fighting with each other, it is the circumstance that people will rely on filial piety and compassionate showing to determine who is on whose side. When the government is corrupt, it is the circumstance that people will declare loyalty to gain affiliation to the power center. (*Wu Qi was the author of Wu Zi Art of War which commanded the same stature as Sun Zi Art of War. Wu Qi was well known as an army general who loved his soldiers so much and made them willing to die for him in any battle. It was all pretended compassion to achieve his selfish political ambition. This story shows that compassion and other morality are often used as tools to fool the people.*)

Verse 19

绝圣弃知 民利百倍 绝仁弃义 民复孝慈 绝巧弃利 盗贼无有

When the country does not prefer brilliant individuals, not opportunistic and use no clever tricks, there will be hundred times more benefit to the people. (*What we want are wise individuals. Clever individuals have deep confidence that they can handle fire and like to play with fire, but they will be burnt once a while. Wise individuals know the danger of fire, use it only when it is necessary and be as discretional as possible. It is important to limit the power of those who can impact the society, in both public and private sectors, to prevent inequality from getting unruly.*) Never demand for compassion and morality, and the society will return to having natural filial piety and compassionate behaviors. (*Filial piety and compassion shall be voluntary in nature and cannot be demanded from anyone, no matter how much we have "invested". Can we regret giving too much love to our children and not getting back the reasonable "return on equity"? It is not a business dealing that is subjected to "buy and sell". It is in the way love is given that matters—not a measure of dollar and cent. Old parents who are loved will naturally be cared for by their children—a good incentive to be loved. Even animals have love for their offspring and parents. It is so natural. Does human need education to acquire the ability to love and reciprocate? When the society has too much desire for filial piety and compassionate values, so much so that these are used to condemn someone for not showing these values, personal liberty will be breached. Confucius said: "I have never seen a real kindhearted person who hates unsympathetic individual. A real kindhearted person is very noble. A person who hates unsympathetic individual may be acting kindhearted merely because he fears being thought an unsympathetic individual." Crave for morality will happen when morality becomes a rare commodity and one can be cheated by faked morality.*) Discourage opportunistic clever tricks and desire for benefit, and there will be no theft and robbery, by legal or illegal means. (*Bankers claim to do good for providing easy loans to "deserving" borrowers who wanted to buy overpriced dream homes and a few million other folks who deserved two homes. The "New Samaritans" suffer the indignity of insolvency and near collapse for their "hard work" but haunted by their "generosity" as regulators hound them into settlement submission, merely for doing God's work. The good news is that tons of underwater homebuyers who are drowning in debt on houses whose prices have fallen 30% to 40% aren't blaming banks and are asking the government to rescue the banks. They didn't realize they were being corralled, like sheep, and they were helping banks fatten their profit pools. This is the danger of wanting compassion like valuable commodity. You can be fished by bait and never realize what was happening.)*

此三言也 以为文未足 故令之有所属 见素抱朴 少私寡欲 绝学无忧

Using the above three principles as guidance may not be sufficient or they may be incorrectly interpreted. So, the spirit that these three principles fall back on need to be defined: we need to be neutral and stay ingenuous (*no preference and no indifference towards brilliant individuals*), have little or no selfishness and desire (*love others unconditionally and never expect anything in return*), and we will have no worries of being tricked even if we don't learn any skills. (*One cannot fall preyed if he has no greed or love for something.*)

Verse 20

唯与诃 其相去几何 美与恶 其相去何若 人之所畏 亦不可以不畏

望呵 其未央才 众人熙熙 若享于太牢 而春登台 我泊焉未佻 若婴儿之未咳

累呵 如无所归 众人皆有余 我独遗 我愚人之心也 惷惷呵 鬻人察察 我独闵闵呵

惚呵 其若海 望呵 其若无所止 众人皆有以 我独顽以鄙 吾欲独异于人 而贵食母

How big is the difference between answering politely to the superior and answering in an impolite way to the subordinate? How big is the difference between beautiful and ugly? We should be wary of the attributes that people dislike, and we shall avoid displaying those attributes to the people. (*Some people don't like the ugly truth, so we should avoid telling them in a blunt manner. There are exceptions where we need not speak the truth when no one wants to hear what we have to say. We may even have to live with certain norms which are not backed by the real truths.*) The psychology of everyday things is very complex and inexhaustible. When everybody is cheerful, like attending a great feast or watching the sights of springtime, I will stay serene and not attract attention, like a baby who is yet to know how to smile. (*Things that most people like to have are not necessarily good. Norms that are commonly accepted as the truths are not necessarily the real truths. We must remind ourselves to be a contrarian and constantly challenge the norms.*) I will behave leisurely, resembling no specific purpose. When everybody has extra to spare, I will stay deprived. My mind is like that of a fool. (*Stay hungry, stay foolish. Don't feel contented, keep learning. But at the same time, like a young child, you should never feel sad that you don't have enough knowledge.*) When everybody tries to portray their brilliance, I will stay dull. Tao is so deep, like the ocean; so wide, like there is no end. Everybody seems to be useful, but I choose to look foolish and ordinary. I choose to be different from everybody and value the kind of life that harmonizes with Tao.

Verse 21
孔德之容 唯道是从

The form of great benevolence changes according to Tao. (*At different time and space, for different group of people, the form of benevolence is different. Some people like socialist system while others like capitalist system.*)

道之物 唯望唯惚 惚呵 望呵 丨丨有象呵 望呵 惚呵 丨丨有物呵 幽
呵 冥呵 丨丨有精呵
其精甚真 其丨丨有信 自今及古 其名不去 以顺众父 吾何以知众
父之然 以此

This thing called Tao is so wide and deep. Although it is deep and wide, there are some appearances that we can observe, and there are some real things that we can discover; (*We can observe the form of milky way, and discover some planets within it but they are all far apart and give the impression that there is nothing else.*) so quiet and dim, but there are some fine qualities that are real and provable. (*The knowledge that we need to deal with everything in this world is so wide and deep. But there are some little-known laws that are really useful and provable.*) Trace backward from what is happening today to those in the past and it never fails to explain precisely the phenomena and their original causes. This is how I could figure out why the original causes or reasons are so. (*We need to understand the fundamental causes or reasons that give rise to the phenomena or what is happening through some provable laws or theories. For the current financial crisis, we could possibly figure out that the cause is excessive risk taking resulting from encouragement and guaranteed bailout by Central Banks. A mathematical model could be developed and applied to the scenario of previous crises to prove the validity of the model.*)

Verse 22

企者不立 自视者不章 自见者不明 自伐者无功 自矜者不长 其
在道也 曰
余食赘行 物或恶之 故有欲者弗居

A person who stands on his toes will not have stable posture. (*Standing on the toes makes the person looks taller but he will easily fall down. A person who portray he is cleverer than he actually is will eventually fail.*) A person who has bloated self-confidence will not rise to prominence. A person who always assumes his view is correct will not get clear insight and is not clever. A person who is puff up with pride will not achieve victory. A person who brags about himself will not be able to keep his position for too long. (*Stay humble, stay foolish.*) From Tao point of view, these behaviors are like left over food or extraneous moves. These behaviors are despised by most people. So, a person who holds higher ambition will not exhibit these behaviors. (*He should display an absence of pride and not be despised by his colleagues or his superior.*)

Verse 23

曲则全 枉则直 洼则盈 敝则新 少则得 多则惑

One will be safe if he is willing to bend instead of taking a hard stand. (*Tree will break amid a strong wind if it refuses to bend. Willingness to consider different views and tweak the original plan will lead to complete solution which takes care of all aspects. In military tactics, the expert approaches his objective indirectly. By selecting a devious and distant route he may march a thousand miles without opposition and attack his enemy unaware.*) One will be able to get thing straight if he is willing to accept that some degree of crookedness is inevitable. (*Tree trunk is not straight but that is alright and it is naturally that way. There is hardly any straight path to get from one place to another. Although the path is crooked, one is able to reach his destination. Rule of laws is good, but villains and fraudulent businessmen have learnt to conceal evidence and are brave to challenge the laws, get away with insufficient evidence to prosecute them. They know how to use crooked way to counter the straight rules. Can we still continue doing what we did and expect better result will somehow emerge? Changes need to be made (to overcome the weakness of the rules being bypassed by clever lawyers) and some degree of overstretch is inevitable. Is the rule of laws trustworthy if petty offences are prosecuted while multimillions frauds defeat the prosecutor and smile all the way to the bank? Whenever there is a comprehensive law, there will always be a lawyer smart enough to get around it. It is easy to put the blame on the prosecutor and the police, but the problems will remain. Is it possible to have enough laws or comprehensive laws to ensure zero crime? Is the problem due to lack of laws? Let the judges do the judging instead of the lifeless book of laws. What is law when there is no more spirit of justice? What is law when the judges cannot be trusted? Rule of laws without civil justice is fascism as opposed to liberalism.*) Swampy terrain could accept water to fill it up. Imperfection will leave room for innovation to improve the state. (*Be receptive for ideas, and don't assume we have the perfect idea.*) Have few desired goals and the plan will be manageable. Being too ambitious and wanting to achieve too many goals will make one lose direction.

是以圣人执·以为天下式 不自视故章 不自见故明 不自伐故有功 弗矜故能长

Great leader will uphold the one law, the most fundamental principle, and become the guide of the world. (*"There is but one law for all, namely that law which governs all law, the law of our Creator, the law of humanity, justice, equity—the law of nature and of nations."—Edmund Burke*) He doesn't act arrogant but accept suggestions to tweak his plan therefore he can become prominent. He doesn't insist on his view but accept other views therefore he can get complete insight of any situations. He doesn't become puffed up with pride therefore he can be careful in his execution of plan and achieve victory. Upon victory, he doesn't brag about it but always be mindful that every challenge requires attentive planning therefore he can continue to overcome every challenge every time. (*Many pre-eminent economists, including former New York Fed President and CEO Tim Geithner, "didn't see the troubling signs" of the U.S. financial crash, until the day it actually happened in 2008, due to deep confidence in economic forecasting models that turned out to be broken, despite numerous warnings from several individuals from as early as year 2000. Hank Paulson, the then US Treasury Secretary, former Chairman and CEO of Goldman Sachs prior to May 2006, declared in July 2007: "This is far and away the strongest global economy I've seen in my business lifetime." Tim Geithner succeeded him as the US Treasury Secretary in January 2009, the classic case of "the worst get on top in politics". The ensuing economic crisis, which is yet to be resolved, shall serve as a negative example of having bloated self-confidence. Unfortunately, the governments and central banks are still helmed by fools who remain convinced they know what they're doing, regardless of how abject their past failures have been.*)

夫唯不争 故莫能与之争 古之所谓曲则全者 几语才 诚全归之

He doesn't compete with anyone on who is more brilliant therefore no one can compete with him. (*A leader could not possibly know more than his subordinates in everything. If he wants to compete with his subordinates, he will surely lose in one aspect to one person and another aspect to another*

38

person. On the contrary, if he doesn't get into competition, no one will be able to claim victory over him. He should instead listen to different opinions and make a decision. A judge cannot at the same time acts as the defense lawyer. When George Washington presided over the Constitutional Convention that drafted the United States Constitution in 1787, he participated little in the debates to maintain collegiality and kept the delegates at their labors, though he did vote for or against the various articles.) The ancient brainy quote of "bend to be safe" is such a wise advice. It really can bring forth safety *(literally as well as in term of safe implementation of plans).*

Verse 24

希言自然 飘风不终朝 暴雨不终日 孰为此 天地而弗能久 而况于人乎

Make as few regulations or instructions as possible and let the people rely on themselves to deal with any problems that they face and live their natural life. *(Napoleon used to leave aside the letters from his subordinates requesting for instruction. By the time he read the letters six months later, the problems were solved. Mao Ze Dong would leave his generals at different parts of China to make their own decisions to deal with the situations they were facing instead of giving specific instructions to them.)* Strong wind does not blow the whole day, and rainstorm does not last for a few days. Why is it so? Even the Nature cannot keep up the force for too long. How much less so the capability of man?

故从事于道者同于道 德者同于德 失者同于失
同于德者 道亦德之 同于失者 道亦失之

A person who works in accordance to Tao harmonizes with Tao. A benevolent person follows benevolent ways. A misguided person views misguided ways as the correct ways. *(We have been educated to believe in misguided ways as the correct ways. For example, people in the business world are told by "Capitalism" propaganda that it is okay to cheat for the sake of making profit. The onus is on the victims to prevent themselves from being cheated. We need to aggressively challenge what we may have accepted as being the truth.*) Tao will bless and be benevolent to the person who follows benevolent ways. Tao will deny success and benevolence to the person who follows misguided ways. (*We have been educated to chase for glory and prosperity. There are limits to how much we can do. A person who defies the Law of Nature and try to do too much on his own, or control everything himself, will find the repercussions the hard ways. An example is Chiang Kai Shek who lost Mainland China to Mao Ze Dong because he tried to micro-manage everything. A person who believes in doing good will be rewarded with good deeds by Tao or the Invisible Hand. A person who does not believe in doing good will have no loyal friend.*)

Verse 25

有物混成 先天地生 萧呵 寥呵 独立而不改 可以为天地母 吾未知其名 字之曰道
强为之名曰大 大曰逝 逝曰远 远曰反

There was a mixture of things before the formation of the sky and the earth. So quiet and so sparse. It was independent and does not change much, and it is the mother of the sky and the earth. I don't know its name. I simply call it Tao, or subjectively designate it as Great. It is so great and has no end. It has no end therefore has far reaching extent. In the far reaching extent, there are repetitions, reverberations, or cycles of flip-sides. (*There was never peace forever. The history is a repeated cycles of peace and chaos, and cause and effect. It does rhythm. The universe is filled with positives and negatives. Since there are repetitions, it is not impossible to study locally and view globally. The various scientific laws can be studied on earth and applied to the universe.*)

道大 天大 地大人亦大
国中有四大 而人居其一焉
人法地 地法天 天法道 道法自然

Tao is great, the sky is great, the earth is great, and the human is also great. The universe has four great things, and the human is one of them. The lives of human (physical and spiritual) are closely related to the earth. The conditions of the earth (wet, dry, grassland, forest, etc.) are closely related to the sky. The conditions of the sky (weather, seasons, rain, wind, etc.) are closely related to Tao. Tao is closely related to the Nature (Physics, Chemistry, Biology, etc.).

Verse 26

重为轻根 静为躁君 是以君子终日行不离其辎重 唯有环馆 燕处
则昭若

若何万乘之主而以身轻天下 轻则失本 躁则失君

The heavy is the foundation of the light. (*Grass grows on steady land. The leader should be steady, not easily influenced, to thwart plan that is not well thought out.*) The calm is the master of the impatience. (*Levees prevent river from flooding the land. The leader should be calm and not go to war upon minor provocation. If one wants to think rationally about a subject, it's wise to get rid of emotional baggage.*) The army general travels all days and never leaves the military supply. While staying in temporary resting place, he will stay calm and not agitated by disturbances. Why would the king of a big country not value his body and go to war lightly? (*During the Warring States period, there were many conflicts between the different states over minor issues. No one actually wins but they make themselves weaker and finally destroyed by the Qin state. Today, many people are hysterical on hearing certain countries are planning to acquire nuclear weapon technology. Has anyone used nuclear weapons in war since World War II? Why not? The reason is no country has gone out of its mind or so stupid to solicit mutually assured destruction (MAD). A good leader should not be hysterical and go to war lightly. There must be some reasons for those countries to feel the need to have nuclear weapons, perhaps as a slingshot to keep the bully of the block at bay. It will be better to make them feel there is no need for such weapons. Even if they are not convinced, "a man cannot be accused of attempting to rape merely because he has the "weapon" to do it". If they didn't physically victimize anybody, no crime is committed and they cannot be prosecuted or oppressed to give up their aspiration for dignity. On the contrary, it will be an evil act to attack them. A law which allows some countries to own nuclear weapons and prohibits others from having it is unfair, and the law shall be null and void.*) Take matter lightly will lose the foundation. Impatient will lose the mastering of the sovereign. (*George Washington proclaimed the USA neutral in the wars raging in Europe after 1793. In his "Farewell Address", again he warned against involvement in foreign wars and "permanent alliances with any portion of the foreign world".*)

Here are the quotes from Jim Rogers (legendary investor and co-founder of Quantum Fund with George Soros, and founder of the Rogers International Commodity Index) on patience and hysteria:

- *One of the best rules anybody can learn about investing is to do nothing, absolutely nothing, unless there is something to do. Most people . . . always have to be playing; they always have to be doing something . . . I just wait until there is money lying in the corner, and all I have to do is go over there and pick it up. I do nothing in the meantime.*
- *When I see hysteria, I usually take a look to see if I shouldn't be going the other way . . . It is amazing how sometimes something important will happen, and the market will keep going despite that. Now, I am experienced enough to know that just because I see something doesn't mean that everyone sees it. A lot of people are going to keep buying or selling just because that has been the thing to do . . . If the market keeps going the way it shouldn't go, especially if it is a hysterical blow off, then you know an opportunity will present itself.*

Verse 27

善行者无辙迹 善言者无瑕谪 善数者不以筹策 善闭者无关楗而不可启也
善结者无绳约而不可解也 是以圣人恒善救人 而无弃人 物无弃财 是谓袭明

A person who is good at traveling will leave no trace. A fine orator will leave no defect in his speech. A skillful mathematician will not need an abacus. An expert at locking will leave no control handle so no one can open the vault. A person who is skillful at tying will leave no knot so no one can untie it. Great leader is good at saving the people (*including rescue and safeguard the people, facilitate productivity improvement, recruit officers and mentoring successor*). He will not give up on anybody. He will not waste resources. This is the long handed down wisdom. (*Different people have different skills. People are the best resources and wealth of a country. Some countries waste their human resources by discouraging the people from reaching their potential but relying on oil and other natural resources to sustain their economy. They risk losing their ability to survive when the natural resources run out or robbed by external forces, literally or through various repression tactics used in the Middle-east since the 1900's.*)

故 善人 善人之师 不善人 善人之资也
不贵其师 不爱其资 虽知乎大迷 是谓眇要

Therefore, good people can be teachers to good people (*in terms of skills as well as morals*). Bad people can serve as reflections or negative examples to good people. He who does not value the teachers and the negative examples is really in great bewilderment even if he is intelligent. This is an important thought.

Verse 28

知其雄 守其雌 为天下溪
为天下溪 恒德不离 恒德不离 复归于婴儿

Knowing you have the strength of the male (*masculine, hard-line, tough, energetic*), but choose to behave like the female (*feminine, soft, tolerance, calm*), and act like the water stream of the world (*provide benefit to all things, never compete with anything, and absorb all unwanted things*). Acting like the water stream of the world, therefore the people are blessed with benevolence and return to the state of non-violent like the baby.

知其荣 守其辱 为天下谷
为天下谷 恒德乃足 恒德乃足 复归于朴

Have the glory, but choose to be humble, and act as the valley of the world (*lie low and be accommodative*). Acting as the valley of the world (*educating the people that puffed up with pride is not a good attribute*), therefore the people are satisfied with benevolence and return to the state of ingenuous. (*Knowing enough is enough will exorcise greed.*)

知其白 守其黑 为天下式
为天下式 恒德不忒 恒德不忒 复归于无极

Knowing that you are innocent, but choose to express guilty and become the role model of the world (*willing to bend instead of taking a hard stand*). Be the role model of the world (*educating the people to be tolerant*), therefore the people will have indefeasible solid base of benevolence and return to the state of non-extremism (*moderation and away from the extreme of self-righteous*). (*When your car is hit by another car in an accident, given the fact that you are not defensive enough to avoid being hit, you should forgive the other driver. After all, you can claim the insurance. Having the rights to do certain thing does not always mean it is correct to exercise the rights. The return may sometime be greater if we exercise self-restraint. Many managers will straightaway accuse the workers of being lazy and inefficient when the required results are not delivered on time. It would be better for the managers to step back and consider whether they are lacking in managerial skills and the workers have been given too many tasks, too little guidance on how to multitask, and too little time. It is the right of China and other countries to build up foreign reserves for self protection against possible lost of economic sovereignty due to external shock. Instead of blaming the exchange rate, it would be better for the USA to acknowledge that their workers are not globally competitive, too many people with skills in non-essential services sector, and find the real solutions to reverse the economic predicaments of high unemployment/underemployment and massive debt.*)

朴散则为器 圣人川之则为官长 大大制无割

Wide-spread ingenuous give rise to development of useful talents (*as oppose to brilliant but greedy individuals*). The great leader recruits them as ministers and the government system will be non-partisan. (*Not divided, agree to disagree, no fighting between different parties or gangs but work together for a common cause. In most democratic governments, the goal of the politicians is to survive the coming election. Politicians will "bribe" the people with all sorts of "benefits" (fiscally irresponsible social welfare, subsidy, economic figures as opposed to real wealth and equality) and "prides" (national, racial, or religious), creating more problems but kick the cans down the road, and finally find a way for someone else to get blamed for it. George Washington was not a member of any political party and hoped that they would not be formed. In his Farewell Address, he warned against the evils of political parties and called for men to serve the common good beyond partisanship.*)

Verse 29

将欲取天下而为之 吾见其弗得已
大天下 神器也 非可为者也
为者败之 执者失之
物或行或随 或嘘或吹 或强或羸 或陪或隳 是以圣人去甚 去太
去奢

If someone plans to conquer and rule the world, I think he will have no way to succeed. The world is a magnificent creation of the Nature. No one can play God and rule it. Those who try to rule the world will fail, and those who try to control it will lose it. (*Look at the Japanese and the Germans in the Second World War.*) Certain people may do it first but taken over by another who follow suit. It may be admired now but condemned at a later time. The empire may appear strong now but weaken later, in peace now but in danger at other time. Therefore the great leader will eliminate extremism, extraordinary ambition, and extravagance. (*Empire begins slowly, building over centuries. This is evident in the Roman Empire, the Russian Empire, and the French Empire. Then the empire either erodes or else it is captured by revolutionaries, as was the case in France (1789-94) and Russia (1917). The reversal is inevitable, although it can be delayed.)*

Verse 30

以道佐人主 不以兵强于天下 其事好还
师之所居 楚棘生之 善者果而已矣 不以取强焉
果而勿娇 果而勿矜 果而勿伐 果而不得已居 是谓果而不强
物壮则老 谓之不道 不道蚤已

A minister who applies Tao in assisting the leader will not support the use of military to conquer the world by force because this kind of action will surely face revenge. (*"War breeds war. Peace breeds prosperity."*) After being occupied by the military, the crops of the land will be destroyed and thorns start to grow. A good leader will only aim at achieving his objective, and never to show off his military strength. Succeed but not feel proud about it; Succeed but not brag about it; Succeed but not puffed up with pride; Succeed merely because there was no other options. This is called succeed without boaster of strength. All things that gain strength will eventually become weaken. Thirst to gain strength does not harmonize with Tao. Not harmonizing with Tao will lead to perish. (*The Chinese foreign policy in the history has always been to have war with no nations; buy peace in exchange for bilateral trade; prepare for war but negotiate for peace. This will not change in the future if the culture is inherited.*)

Verse 31

夫兵者 不祥之器也 物或恶之 故有欲者弗居
君子居则贵左 用兵则贵右 故兵者 非君子之器也
兵者 不祥之器也 不得已而用之
铦袭为上 勿美也 若美之 是乐杀人也
夫乐杀人 不可以得志于天下矣 是以吉事上左 丧事上右 是以偏将军居
左 上将军居右 言以丧礼居之也 杀人众 以悲哀泣之 战胜 以丧礼处之

The military is an inauspicious tool. This entity is disliked by most people. So, a person who holds higher ambition will hope not ever need to use

46

it. (*Ancient Chinese denoted left-hand side as Yang which means sunny or lively; and right-hand side as Ying, which means gloomy or lackluster.*) The ministers prefer peace and keep to the left-hand side (*to do "sunny" works that promote livelihood*). The army generals will take the right-hand side (*to be reminded to stay "gloomy" and don't plan to use the military for killing*). The military is not a tool that the ministers like to use. The military is an inauspicious tool. It shall only be used when there is really no other option. It is best to make surprise attack with sharp weapons. (*Emperor Liu Xiu of middle Han Dynasty was a good role model of Tao practitioner and he was excellent at surprise attack. Just when the enemy thought that his troop was 40 times smaller and he was fearful, he would charge forward and cripple the enemy without having to kill large number of soldiers because the enemy collapsed by domino effect. Sun Zi said: "Therefore at first be shy like a maiden. When the enemy gives us an opening, be swift as a hare and they will be unable to oppose us."*) Don't sing praise for the victory. Otherwise, it would imply that the military likes to kill people. A government which likes to kill people will not be able to gain respect from the world. (*Causing non-combatant casualties is simply unintelligent; it's bad public relations and doesn't make friends in any quarter, although morality is never a consideration in battlefield.*) Auspicious occasions take the sunny left-hand side. Funeral takes the gloomy right-hand side. Therefore, army assistant general takes the left-hand side while the chief general takes the right-hand side. This is to symbolize that going to war shall apply ceremony akin to funeral. When many enemy soldiers are killed, the military shall hold condolence ritual for the dead. Upon victory, the military shall hold funeral ceremony for the dead.

Verse 32

道恒无名 朴虽小 而天下弗敢臣 侯王若能守之 万物将自宾 天地相合 以俞甘露 民莫之令 而自均焉

The true Tao has no name and not famous. Although being ingenuous is just a small part of Tao, the world will dare not dispute it. If the king can remain ingenuous, naturally all things will admire and become allegiance to him. When the sky and the earth come together, rain will drizzle. (*When water vaporizes from earth and form clouds in the sky, we get rain. When the people and the government cooperate closely, everybody benefits. No external force will be able to invade and occupy the country, not forever.*) The people need not be instructed and they will naturally do their part for the country and achieve equality naturally.

始制有名　名亦既有　夫亦将知止　知止所以不殆
俾道之在天下也　猷川谷之于江海也

Every system created is given a name. Once it has a name, we shall recognize that it has its limit. Knowing the limit is vital to avoid danger. (*Ingenuous is a good way but it has its limit. For example, the enemy may use guile against our guileless. If one recognizes the limit, he can then find ways to cover the limit, such as employing talented but humble ministers in the government, or form alliance with another country.*) This small part of Tao (referring to ingenuous practice) compared to the sky and the earth is like creek compared to the sea. (*There is no simple answer to complex problem. When a theory is developed and given a name, it will have limitations. These limitations must be identified and managed accordingly. The financial crisis in the USA and Europe is terrifying the whole world. Some economists blame it on free market economy while others blame it on government central planning and intervention. Who is right? Both arguments are probably right, but both extremes are wrong. Free market economy has never been fully embraced by any country. The importance of free markets advocated by Hayekian has remained a theoretical construct and assumed to have limitations in the real world. There were always varying degrees of government central planning and intervention. Keynesian ideas of government fiscal policy and central bank monetary policy actions are the examples. On the other hand, free market concepts have frequently been misused in making real world policy choices. An example is the decades long of deregulation mismanagement which encouraged excessive risk taking to maximize profit, both to the banks and the governments. As a result, government debt and household debt have escalated to a dangerous level worldwide. Too much money has been printed to "stimulate" the economy due*) *to misguidance that economic growth can only be sustained by ever increasing consumption with borrowing and little saving. This is a misuse of Keynesian theory to intervene in almost everything. Deficit spending by the government, in good time as well as in bad time, and often favors the politically connected businessmen, has led to widen rich-poor gap as well as the current tipping point of a global economic collapse. Inflation and devaluation of fiat money further transfer the wealth of the nation to the rich. GDP figures have been inflated by virtual wealth, and yet some economists continue to call for more debt to solve the debt crisis. Common sense tells us it is insane to do the same thing over and over again and expecting different results. Can this time be different? It is astonishing that the markets keep asking the Central Banks to break the rules in the name of restoring market confidence and saving the economy. The reliance on the assumption that the market is efficient and knows best appears to have dulled our awareness of the risks building up in the financial markets over the last few decades. Hedge funds have been cashing on the inefficiency of the markets. Totally no regulation is ignorant of the risks. Failure in regulating reckless or imprudent practices in the private financial services industry is failure in protecting the properties of the people (as in inflation and devaluation of fiat money, transfer of wealth of the nation to the rich, widening the rich-poor gap). On the other hand, too much regulation on regular banking system will push money into the under-regulated shadow banking institutions or the black market. Some regulations are providing unfair advantages to the big players compared to smaller banks that carry out honest conventional business, forcing them to become uncompetitive. There must be a balance between Keynesian and Hayekian economic theories. It is an art analogy to what makes a chef great. The government must be wise to apply the policy mix, minimize intervention, and step aside for the free markets to work. "Whether it is black cat or white cat, the one which catches rats is the good cat."—Deng Xiao Ping. We must not have a system for the sake of having a system but make progressive changes to keep pace with the changing needs. Never be too fanatic to adhere to one ideology. But one thing for sure is pushing excess consumption doesn't cause the real economy to grow. To paraphrase, it is productivity that creates wealth. Policies aimed at encouraging consumption, instead of increasing production, are what turned the savings rate negative and resulted in the huge sovereign debt issues in the supposedly rich countries. It is stupid to prop up GDP numbers with wasteful consumption; it counts wealth consumption and destruction as wealth production. The fundamental accounting flaw is so absurd. It is missing the forest for the trees. Commonsense tells us we must produce more than we consume or perish. Overproduction must be avoided. When the people and the government consume the excess outputs of overproduction, using bank loan and credit card debt, they will become poorer; only the GDP numbers and the purse of the rich are growing. Government guaranteed obligations and national debt, held by the public and the government, are the liabilities of the people, and the detrimental effects will be felt on the days of reckoning.)*

Verse 33

知人者 知也 自知者 明也 胜人者 有力也 自胜者 强也 知足者
富也
强行者 有志也 不失其所者 久也 死而不忘者 寿也

He who can judge the talent and character of others is intelligent. He who knows his own strength and weakness is wise. He who defeats others has physical strength. He who defeats his own weakness is the real strongman. He who is contented with his life is rich. (*Many people became slaves to money, many just couldn't accept that many things do not matter in life, until the moment before they die to discover that they had never lived. Are those things money can buy (power, status, woman, expensive fashions and foods, etc.) really worth the troubles of chasing money? The fun of living is in the process, not in the ending. What we accumulated at the end does not matter to us, even if it goes with us into our grave. The fun of eating is when the food is in our mouth, not after it ended up in our rectum.*) He who pursues something with determination has willpower. He who doesn't lose his principle or foundation will last long. He who is not forgotten after death lives forever.

Verse 34

道泛分 其可左右也 成功遂事而弗名有也
万物归焉而弗为主 则恒无欲也 可名于小
万物归焉而弗为主 可名于大
是以圣人之能成大也 以其不为大也 故能成大

Tao is everywhere. It can influence the progress of everything. It sometime gives rise to victory and success without our knowledge (*and not given the credit*). All things in the universe have their own destiny and not dictated by Tao. Tao has no desire or feeling. (*Tao does not love or hate anything, therefore it doesn't care if one wins or loses; succeeds or fails.*) Some may say it has little role (*when they don't feel any significant influence from Tao*). Tao allows all things in the universe to be responsible for their own destiny and give them total freedom. Some may say it is magnanimous. (*In a country with liberal government, some people may feel the government has done little to help them. Others may feel the government is magnanimous for not restricting their freedom with unnecessary regulations and gives rise to their success through competition and innovation.*) The great leader can become great because he doesn't plan to accumulate big achievements using government resources. (*If a leader wishes to accumulate big achievements with his own two-hands, he can only achieve mediocre outcomes. He must step aside and let the people do their parts to bring forth the most benefit to the country, and he will be remembered as the great leader who presided over the great achievements. He must give the people total freedom to excel with their own efforts rather than making regulations to unnecessarily control the people's behavior. China's market-oriented reform, carried out steadily and with considerable care, is a great example.*) Hence, he can bring forth great achievements to the country and the people. (*No intervention is the strategy; big achievement is the final objective. Let the history speaks louder than the actions. This is the main ingredient which brings forth the success of Great Britain and the USA. The spending of the government should be limited and tax on the people and corporations should be minima. As the US Congressman Dr. Ron Paul suggests: "Let the people spend the money rather than the government. Taking the money out of the hand of the government doesn't mean the money isn't going to be spent. The individual is going to spend it. People will start to invest again and building automobiles or other things. It is where the money being spent that is more important. The money is not taken away but put into productive use. Government spending the money is non-productive. It goes into bureaucracy, regulations, subsidizing corporations that don't deserve to be subsidized, and bailing out people. That's all wasteful spending. That damages the economy. You want the money to be spent by individual and business people but not the government. On government-funded medical R&D, money is often spent on political reason rather than market reason. Lobbyists like drug companies come in and they line up. Decision is made by politicians and bureaucrats rather than by the market place. If you want more R&D spending, it will be better directed if investors and the market make this decision. The politicians and bureaucrats aren't smart enough to know exactly what you should be investing in, which immunity you have to give. When government makes a mistake, it hurts everybody. If a business makes a mistake in R&D, it hurts only that company. The reliability on government to make decision is the cause of the problems in recent years.")*

Verse 35

执大象 天下往 往而不害 安平泰 乐与饵 过客止 故道之出言
曰 淡呵其无味也
视之 不足见也 听之 不足闻也 用之 不可既也

Possessing the image of a great country (*in terms of people friendly rather than military hegemony*), all things in the world will admire and migrate to the country. When immigrants are not harmed, there will be peace and prosperity. (*People will migrate toward the least predatory states where they could enjoy the most freedom, and create the most wealth for themselves and their posterity. Countries struggling to persuade their citizens to come home ought to reflect on the push factors the governments have created rather than blaming the pull factors from other countries. Governments should compete for citizens, which would lead to more places where people can live as they want. It could become a worldwide revolution fought and won without guns. Of course, robbers and conmen who prey on decent people are not welcomed. This* can be managed by effective and efficient law enforcements to uphold justice in the country. But for practical reason, citizenship limit need to be set because a country cannot accommodate more people than the land can support and provide.) The happiness and plentiful environment will make traveler stay. Talk about Tao tastes dull (because it advocates do nothing, unless there is something to do, unlike other philosophies that suggest the government to play with cleverness and do various things. Playing is always interesting compared to staying serene but it may not be good for long-term well-being.) It can barely be seen and heard. But when it is used, it is inexhaustible.

Verse 36

将欲歙之 必古张之 将欲弱之 必古强之 将欲去之 必古兴之 将
欲夺之 必古与之
是谓微明

Some characteristics of Tao are: when it wants something to contract, it will first let it expand. (Bubble expands and then burst into nothing.) When it wants something to weaken, it will first let it gain strength. (Empires gain strength, become bloated, and finally collapse on own blunder.) When it wants something to wither, it will first let it flourish. (Bankers become rich, take more risks, and finally go bankrupt on their own greed.) When it wants to snatch something from someone, it will first give him more things to hold. (Politicians want to do too many things only to fail doing anything right.) This is the hidden truth. (In the last decade central banks worldwide, led by USA Federal Reserve Bank, have printed too much money and kept interest rates too low. Money has flooded into the emerging markets, especially the favored BRICs; acronym for Brazil, Russia, India and China. The result has been a surge of corruption in all four BRICs, accompanied by a surge in mal-investment, leading to housing bubbles that is entirely misdirected and a waste of resources. The governments arrogantly claim credit for the resulting GDP growth without realizing the impending risk of economic collapse. The wasted resources will not generate income but become unproductive inventory during the recession years. The GDP growth in the prior years becomes meaningless overnight. A 2008-style banking collapse seems inevitable. It *will be a great "learning experience" for the electorates on how government overspending damages the economy.*)

柔弱胜刚强 鱼不脱于渊 邦利器不可以示人

Soft and defensive people can defeat hard and offensive aggressors. (*We can take a soft and non-confrontational stand against strong enemies to make them bloated with pride. We will not need to apply much force against them as they will then collapse on their blunder. In facing an invading enemy, avoid toe-to-toe contact with the enemy but use asymmetric tactics. As Mao Ze Dong said, we retreat when the enemy advances; we advance when the enemy retreats.*) Fish will not come out of deep river and get caught by fisherman. The special weapons of the country cannot be unveiled to the enemy. (*The defense forces should not leave their fort to combat the enemy on a disadvantageous ground. The military shall use sharp weapons to launch surprise attack against the enemy.*)

Verse 37
道恒无名 侯王若能守之 万物将自化
化而欲作 吾将阗之以无名之朴 夫将不辱 不辱以静 天地将自正

The true Tao has no name and not celebrated. If the king can uphold the practice of Tao, all things will resolve by themselves. When there is nothing else to resolve and the king started to have ambition to do something to disturb the status quo (*or have obsession for entertainment and lavish lifestyle*), I will tame it with the ingenuous principle of not becoming celebrity. (*Less cooperation of any sort given to the government, paying less tax or doing no patriotic duty, will result in less mischief it can get into. As Gandhi showed us, civil disobedience can not only be an ethical choice, but a very powerful force for change.*) Not celebrated therefore there will be no insult of losing the fame (*due to failure in carrying out plan that is not really necessary in the first place*). No insult is the result of quietness (*do nothing, absolutely nothing, unless there is something to do*). The world will become just right by itself. (*Give freedom to individuals to do what they want and innovate different ideas as they wish. There is no need for a celebrity leader to unite the people thinking, direct the people toward certain goals, or plan everything for the people. One million brains are definitely better than one brain. As Doug Casey (the author of the best selling book "Crisis Investing" and the founder and chairman of Casey Research) once said, "Being united amounts to groupthink; it caters to the lowest common denominator. Uniting around a political leader is a symptom of moral bankruptcy. What made America great was individuals thinking and acting as individuals." The sole purpose of bringing success to one's country is for the fortune and happiness of all citizens. It is meaningless to be a military or financial hegemony of the world if the people are generally weak in terms of mental strength (no critical thinking) and personal wealth (not able to rely on themselves) because they are each controlled by the power-that-be to perform the predefined tasks (threaten other people or other country, vote for the politicians who threaten them with force or withdrawal of generosity) for the illusory glory of the country.)*

Only The Mother-Earth Can Save The People

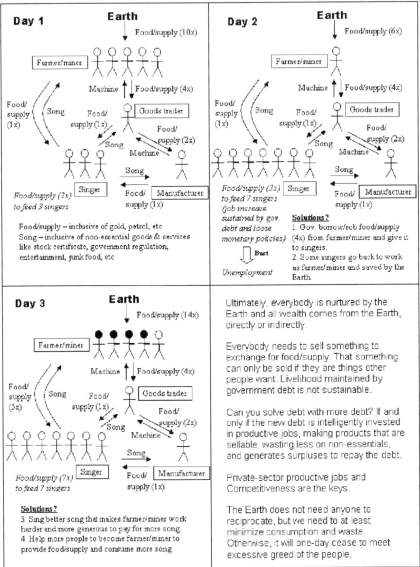

Day 1

Earth — Food/supply (10x)

Farmer/miner

Machine — Food/supply (4x)

Food/supply (1x) — Song — Food/supply (1x) — Goods trader

Food/supply (2x)

Song — Machine

Song

Food/supply (3x) to feed 3 singers — Singer — Food/supply (1x) — Manufacturer

Food/supply – inclusive of gold, petrol, etc
Song – inclusive of non-essential goods & services like stock certificate, government regulation, entertainment, junk food, etc

Day 2

Earth — Food/supply (6x)

Farmer/miner

Machine — Food/supply (4x)

Food/supply (1x) — Song — Food/supply (1x) — Goods trader

Food/supply (2x)

Song — Machine

Song

Food/supply (3x) to feed 7 singers (job increase sustained by gov. debt and loose monetary policies) — Singer — Food/supply (1x) — Manufacturer

Bust

Unemployment

Solutions?
1. Gov. borrow/rob food/supply (4x) from farmer/miner and give it to singers.
2. Some singers go back to work as farmer/miner and saved by the Earth

Day 3

Earth — Food/supply (14x)

Farmer/miner

Machine — Food/supply (4x)

Food/supply (5x) — Song — Food/supply (1x) — Goods trader

Food/supply (2x)

Song — Machine

Song

Food/supply (7x) to feed 7 singers — Singer — Food/supply (1x) — Manufacturer

Solutions?
3. Sing better song that makes farmer/miner work harder and more generous to pay for more song.
4. Help more people to become farmer/miner to provide food/supply and consume more song.

Ultimately, everybody is nurtured by the Earth and all wealth comes from the Earth, directly or indirectly.

Everybody needs to sell something to exchange for food/supply. That something can only be sold if they are things other people want. Livelihood maintained by government debt is not sustainable.

Can you solve debt with more debt? If and only if the new debt is intelligently invested in productive jobs, making products that are sellable, wasting less on non-essentials, and generates surpluses to repay the debt.

Private-sector productive jobs and Competitiveness are the keys.

The Earth does not need anyone to reciprocate, but we need to at least minimize consumption and waste. Otherwise, it will one-day cease to meet excessive greed of the people.

How Wall Street Earn Trillions from Turning Papers Around When No Real Tangible Product Is Made?

Where does the money come from? It is due to Money Multiplication effect of Fractional Reserve Banking system. For every dollar that the Central Bank created, commercial banks are able to multiply the money supply by many times and put into circulation. Wall Street bankers, hedge fund managers and stock traders have been able to suck the newly created money into their pockets. The more money is electronically created, the value of the currency is more diluted. Effectively, the money is stolen from the people without their knowledge since their saving can now buy fewer things. Everything seems to become more expensive. Businesses are forced to increase profit margin in order to keep their head above the water. Unions demand for higher pay for the same reason. Eventually the competitiveness of the citizen compared to other countries is destroyed.

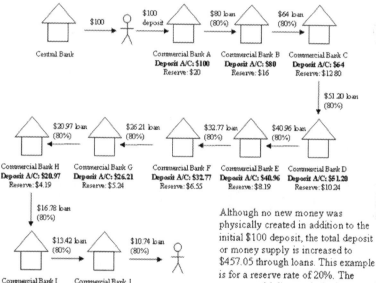

Although no new money was physically created in addition to the initial $100 deposit, the total deposit or money supply is increased to $457.05 through loans. This example is for a reserve rate of 20%. The money multiplier, m, is the inverse of the reserve requirement, R:

$$m = \frac{1}{R}$$

If the reserve requirement R is 10%, the money supply can be increased to $1000 through loans in the market.

Total Amount of Deposit: $457.05
Total Reserve: $89.26
Total Reserve + Last Amount lent out = $100, i.e.
 the original amount

Government Intervention Causes Increasing Medical Cost

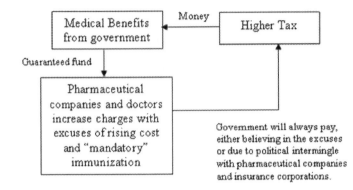

By raising the prices of new drugs and devices literally tenfold, government-funded medical benefit probably kills more people every year than those who are saved.

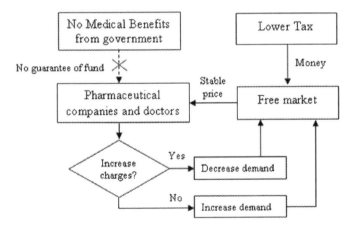

In a free market, medical costs should be expected to fall, like the cost of most technology.

PART II

TE [德]

Verse 38

上德不德 是以有德 下德不失德 是以无德
上德无为 而无以为也 下德为之 而有以为
上仁为之 而无以为也 上义为之 而有以为也
上礼为之 而莫之应也 则攘臂而扔之

The best form of benevolence is needs no benevolence, because there is plenty of benevolence around. The worst benevolence is striving not to lose the last drop of benevolence, because benevolence is in scarcity. (*When the society is peaceful and everyone feels happy to rely on himself, each is free to make anything for a living without regulatory bureaucracy, there is no need for benevolence from anybody, much less the government. When the government tries to be a benevolent nanny, it means that the government feels there is not enough benevolence in the society. For a country that has been ruled for more than a century, the fact that benevolence hand-out is still needed would be a big slap on the face of the government. It would be even worst when new laws need to be passed so that the people know how to behave because it means the government has made the society more chaotic so much so that the older generation did not need such laws.*) The best benevolence is needs no intervention and there is no big objective to achieve. (*The best economy is one which needs no fiscal stimulus.*) The inferior benevolence is when the government have to embark on ambitious policies and there seems to be endless problems to be solved. Compassion can be made the top priority in government policy, providing welfare to the society, when there is no specific target to achieve or no big problem to be solved. (*This is the case when the government can afford to give generously and not expecting any form of returns or any behavioral compliance such as gratitude. Social welfare package will please the people but it is not sustainable. It is better to let the people decide their own destiny and make their own saving to face rainy days and retirement rather than giving them the false sense of security and led them to go all out to consume too much, again and again, and borrow to do it. If one chooses inaction for retirement providence, it is his freedom of choice, after all no one can guarantee that he will live beyond retirement age to need any pension scheme. It is authoritarianism to rule that the people are not capable of taking care of themselves and therefore the government must mandate them to make saving in a Ponzi Social Security scheme. While the sincerity and true intention of the mandate are questionable, the certainty is the scheme dulls the peoples' awareness of risk of losing self-reliant capability as well as all the promised welfare when the government suddenly goes bankrupt, like what is happening in some of the European countries. This is the danger of being addicted to compassion policy: lost of self-reliant capability as a consequence of being told that you cannot possibly be responsible for yourselves and you need the government to look after you; lost of freedom, liberty and property to the politicians and their cronies; view the government as God for compassion and mercy; view compassion as valuable commodity and fooled by hypocritical politicians who pretend to champion compassion values. Anybody can be generous using someone else money. Politicians are using the people's money, through natural resources, taxes and national debt, to buy the people's votes. And the people are thrilled about the "generosity". Politicians use free money to gain tons of personal benefits. Which politician wouldn't do it when the people approve the practice? When the day of reckoning comes, the people will have to pay for the borrowed prosperity. If a robber steals $2 million from the public and then donates $1 million for charity in which you are one of the beneficiaries, do you have the moral obligation to be grateful to him? The problem is many* *people would and they don't care where and how the "philanthropist" gets the money. Affirmative actions have made the blacks lazier, dependent upon generosity, rather than elevating their social status. There is a conspiracy theory suggesting this outcome is intentional by the white policy makers to cement the blacks to the bottom as poor people. In oil-rich countries with zero tax, government generosity becomes unsustainable when food prices increase multifold and sparks social unrest due to the government's failure to continue playing God. "And having looked to Government for bread, on the very first scarcity they will turn and bite the hand that fed them."—Edmund Burke. "Perhaps the fact that we have seen millions voting themselves into complete dependence on a tyrant has made our generation understand that to choose one's government is not necessarily to secure freedom."—Friedrich August von Hayek. If the government really cares about the people, the best thing it can do for them is to push for totally free markets. That makes it both necessary and rewarding for the people to learn valuable skills and to become creators of value, as opposed to being burdens on society. If some people choose to produce less, they must be ready to earn less and consume less; they should not feel envy of others who live a more plentiful life. No one should criticize the way of life they choose to live or help them solve the "problem" they don't perceive as an unbearable problem. It is unfair to expect our neighbor to give us some money just because they have higher income. Similarly, it is unfair to impose higher tax on people who work harder to earn more just because they can afford to do so.)* Justice will need to be made the top priority in government policy, making various laws to prevent crimes because the people cannot be trusted, when some key performance indexes need to be scrutinized and there seems to be endless social problems to be solved. (*The state where justice and compassion are needed is definitely not as good as the state when benevolence is not perceived as a need. However, when reality dictates that the society is not ready for the best benevolence, we will have to settle for the second or third class benevolence. Poverty and backwardness will leave no dignity to the country and it will be at risk of being bullied by external forces. Look at the fate of the Middle-East Ottoman Empire and China before 1940s. But a good leader shall know the ultimate state to attain and enshrine the vision in the Constitution. China's transition to a market economy, carried out steadily and with considerable care, should serve as a good example. In raising children, we need to first teach them some manners to follow but not too much and not expecting them to be able to appreciate the needs for those rituals. When they are old enough or have reached the state of mind to understand reasons, we can start imposing rules and discipline on the children with regards to justice, justifying what is right and what is wrong. Beyond teenage, we can be compassionate and generous in giving every assistances to them without expecting any forms of return, including satisfactory college results to please the parents. The children should be matured enough to appreciate the concept of reciprocity and importance of relating to each other voluntarily in a society. Beyond college age, we have to set them free and let them be responsible for themselves; allow them to make good decisions as well as bad ones and learn from mistakes. Let them be proud to declare that they achieve what they aspired for by themselves. That is the ultimate state of benevolence. It would be impractical to expect a baby to need no intervention to survive on herself, but it is ridiculous for teenager to require spoon-feeding unless he is a handicap. If we love our children, we will want them to have the capability to face challenges of the cruel real world rather than giving them the impression that we will provide for all their needs forever. Like driving a car, we don't want to be stuck on the first gear throughout the journey.)* A government which makes ritual the top priority, forcing the people to comply with various behavioral traits and follow strict protocols, will find that the people do not respond to such complex system and the government will have to raise its arm and force the people to conform. (*This is related to Verse 17 which says "The best government is one that the people know it existed but doesn't feel its interference. The second best government is one that the people love and praise it. The third is government that the people fear it. And the worst is government that the people hate and despise." "In effect, to follow, not to force the public inclination; to give a direction, a form, a technical dress, and a specific sanction, to the general sense of the community, is the true end of legislature."—Edmund Burke*)

故 失道而后德 失德而后仁 失仁而后义 失义而后礼
大礼者 忠信之薄也 而乱之首也
前识者 道之华也 而愚之首也
是以大丈夫居其厚而不居其薄 居其实而不居其华 故去彼而取此

In summary, lost of Tao lead to prioritization of benevolence; lost of benevolence lead to prioritization of compassion; lost of compassion lead to prioritization of justice; lost of justice lead to prioritization of ritual. (*The USA used to be a truly free country, with personal liberty placed above anything else, and everybody thinks and acts as individual. That little house on the prairie did not need any government help, but thank God for escaping government disturbance. That was the state of benevolence. Then came someone who wanted to be known as a hero and started social welfare scheme, unemployment compensation, Medicare and Medicaid, mandatory vaccination, foreign aid, and other "compassionate" schemes to meddle around the natural life of the people. While the sincerity and true intention of the schemes are debatable, it is undisputable that among the beneficiaries are the pharmaceutical companies, health care industries, insurance corporations, bankers, politicians, as well as military-industrial complex because the demanded military ally (i.e. allow setting up of naval bases) as repayment for the foreign aid causes subsequent ballooning of defense spending. Large profits flow to armaments companies. A portion of the profits reflow into campaign contributions to "the people's representatives" in Washington D.C. and to presidential candidates who openly sell out their country to private interests. The unwelcomed international meddling angers some people and lead to terrorist attacks on Americans. The Patriot Act was passed and distorted criminal acts of violence into acts of war; and now the Congress approves the 2012 National Defense Authorization Act which legalizes martial law to literally arrest American citizens and detain them in prison indefinitely without trial on "suspected" ties to terrorists. The country has entered the state of Justice.*) Ritual is emphasized when loyalty and trust became superficial, and it is the prime factor which leads to chaos. (*When everybody pretends to be religious followers of the ritual, everybody is actually fooling each other without any sincere loyalty and trust. When people in higher position demand show of respect for their sheer position instead of their good deeds to earn the due respect, they will get it but without any sincerity element in it.*) Those who foretell the future and prescribe policies for the people to follow are actually only painting or promising a beautiful scenario of Tao. They are in fact the prime factor which leads to stupidity. (*Nobody really knows what will happen in the future and the purported outcomes of any ritual system may well be empty promises. When everybody religiously obeys the ritual (religious, cultural, economic, and/or political systems), no questioning of the establishment, no one will be innovative to think out-of-the-box for creative improvement of civilization. Of course, unity will make it easy for the leader to dictate and accomplish whatever he wishes, for good or for bad reasons. The people may feel it is good to unite under one political leader so that they can continue to play dumb and dull to any surrounding risk, under the false impression that the almighty leader will handle everything. The leader may well take the people in the wrong direction and on a road to perdition. Like the movie "The Matrix", all men and women are plugged into the Matrix and receive constant stream of stimulant from the Intelligent Mind to live in an imaginary world of wonderful dream and ignorant of the rotten real world; any man who tries to wake everybody up will be hunted down or disliked by people who prefer not to wake up but continue to live in the dream. However, history has shown that no human can resist the temptation of having huge power; leaders will eventually be lured to the dark side or have their power captured by lobbyists. A good leader who truly loves his country will not want to amass too much power for himself. One fine example is George Washington, the first President of the USA.*) Hence, a man of dignity would choose to live where ingenuous benevolence exists (*personal liberty and self-reliant*) and not succumb to lure of superficial compassion and rite (*where certain degrees of freedom and privacy must be sacrificed*); to live where the true substance of benevolence exist (*sincerity in human relation and non-interference*) and not fooled by artificial prosperity (*spending with borrowing and false promises of social security*). This is why a great leader rejects the lower-quality benevolence and chooses to provide the environment of best benevolence.

Verse 39

昔之得一者 天得一以清 地得一以宁 神得一以灵 谷得一以盈
万物得一以生 侯得一以为天下正

Those who master the one law, the most fundamental principle of Tao, in
the past (*related to Verse 14*) observed that: the sky being clear (*no obstacle
all the way to outer space*) is in line with Tao; the earth being steady is
in line with Tao; the Nature being productive is in line with Tao; the
valley being full of lives is in line with Tao; all things being in line with
Tao to survive; the king being in line with Tao and the country become
just. (*Everything is what it is because Tao made it that way; each has their
natural and unique characteristics. Knowing the characteristics of the four
seasons gives one the clarity of how to deal with the weather changes; knowing
the characteristics of the earth leads one to find a safe place to settle down; the
Nature obeys the natural laws and produces different species at different places;
the valley is naturally suitable to nurture all kinds of life forms; all things
follow their own natural way to live, requiring no one to tell them how to live
their lives; the king leaves the people to make anything for a living, collects
little tax, and there will be no demand for social welfare. If the king dictates
that no one eats meat but vegetable for uniformity sake, tigers and lions will
surely protest against the ruling. "There is but one law for all, namely that law
which governs all law, the law of our Creator, the law of humanity, justice,
equity—the law of nature and of nations."—Edmund Burke*)

其致之也 谓天毋已清 将恐裂 谓地毋已宁 将恐废 谓神毋已灵
将恐歇 谓谷毋已盈 将恐竭 谓万物毋已生 将恐灭 谓侯王毋已
贵以高 将恐蹶

By induction, the sky will have risk of cracking if it is not clear; (*Violating
the natural laws can be devastating. Relying on artificial floating sunshade
in the sky for protection against solar flare and cosmic rays is destined to fail.
It is better to refrain from destroying the natural shield. Technologies damage
the environment and create more business opportunities for new technologies
to be innovated to repair the old damages and make new damages. Synthetic*

medicines kill some germs but create more dangerous mutated germs for newer medicines to be innovated to kill the increasing variants of germs and provide businesses to pharmaceutical companies and the related industries, including bankers and insurance corporations. It is a vicious cycle. We benefit from technologies but we also sacrifice a lot of things. It is a zero-sum game. It is better to be moderate.) the earth will have risk of collapsing if it is not steady; the Nature will have risk of destruction if it is not productive; the valley will have risk of becoming a desert if it is not full of lives; all things will have risk of extinction if they lose their ability to make a living; the king will have risk of being toppled if he does not treat the support of the people with great importance.

故 必贵而以贱为本 必高矣而以下为基 夫是以 侯王自谓 孤 寡 不谷 此其贱之本与 非也? 故致数舆无舆 是故不欲禄禄若玉 珞 珞若石

Highly regarded things are sustained by abundant of cheap things; (*A one-hundred dollar bill is made up of 10,000 unworthy one-cent coins. A country is made up of millions of people and not a single one can be sacrificed unless he voluntarily wants to do so to show his love for others. Respect and treat all people like they are equally important. Even though a sold-ier has sold himself to his country, his life is at the mercy of the commanding officer in national defence missions, no soldier can be simply sacrificed like a pawn on a chess board.*) High position must have support from the foundation. (*Mountain cannot reach the sky without a broad base. A leader must value the contributions of his subordinates with respect no matter how small are those contribution. In Higglytown, everyone is a hero.*) Hence, the king addresses himself as "orphan", "widower" or "unworthy". Isn't this a display of not undervalue the position of the lower ranks? (*The ancestors knew the dangers of addresses or titles which represent inflated reputation or position. Unfortunately, the hypocritical addresses have fallen into the trap of ritual after a few generations when the original spirit no longer alive although the king continues to use the pitiful addresses. George Washington was careful to make sure that the titles and trappings for him were suitably republican and*

LAO ZI PHILOSOPHY OF LIBERAL GOVERNMENT

never emulated European royal courts. Instead of the more majestic names suggested, he preferred the title "Mr. President".) The best tribute is no need for tribute. (Step aside and let the Nature takes its own course. That is the best benevolence as opposed to itchy hands that always have to be doing something to solve problem that doesn't exist with "solution" that is the cause of the problem.) Therefore, it is not desirable to be beautiful like jade (artificial sculpting) but preferably to stay naturally shaped and hard like rock.

Verse 40

上士闻道 堇能行之 中士闻道 若存若亡 下士闻道 大笑之
弗笑不足以为道 是以建言有之曰 明道如费 进道如退 夷道如类
上德如谷 大白如辱 广德如不足 建德如偷 质真如渝 大方无隅
大器免成 大音希声 大象无形 道褒无名 夫唯道 善始且善成

When highly talented individuals hear about Tao, they will endeavor to practice it; when moderately talented individuals hear about Tao, they will adopt some parts and doubt the others; (*Many economists agree that free-market system is the best but no country has ever pushed for totally free markets. There are always some government interventions in the name of Keynesianism. The faith in Hayekian and Mises concepts of free-market economy is lacking.*) When low intelligence or untalented individuals hear about Tao, they will laugh. (*Being able to see the moon cannot be considered as having farsighted vision. If Tao is a common knowledge, it does not need Lao Zi to talk about it. Some economists laugh about the "stupidity" of classical Gold Standard by simply brushes aside the tremendous economic growth in 1879-1913 when nearly every major currency was tied to gold. They are oblivious to the currency devaluation since 1971 and the financial crisis of 2008 caused by fiat money. When you sell your produce, will you accept payment in the form of casino chip printed with the US flag? The implicit statement from the casino chip issuer is: "Trust me! You can surely exchange it for casino chip printed with the flag of any country. But it is not a guarantee that you can redeem back your produce with the same casino chip". The issuer can issue as many casino chips as he likes, using phony justifications. With Gold Standard, the issuer will have to exchange valuable things for gold before he can issue a casino chip. Gold is dug out from the Earth, like any other rare earth used in technological applications, but its use is for making of coins. Its price is determined by market forces: labor for digging versus available wealth in the society. If nobody has extra wealth to pay for new gold extracted, the price of gold will decrease. Gold miners will suffer the same fate as miners of other commodities. It is so stupid to think that paper and ink are more valuable than gold. Why should we victimize the miners and benefit the "casino"? Only the accomplices of the "casino" will stop the return to Gold Standard. It will be the end of the derivatives market, which Warren Buffett calls it financial weapon-of-mass-destruction, because Gold Standard will make commodity prices stable and it will be difficult for speculators to manipulate the markets and cause large price fluctuation to profit from it. For your saving in the bank, what is the benefit of being paid 5% interest with newly printed papers that actually cause the purchasing power to reduce by more than 10%? The net interest is negative. Thorsten Polleit explains that "collective corruption" is the reason why returning to sound money faces such high, perhaps insurmountable, hurdles once fiat money has been put into place and public opinion accepts adherence to the fraudulent scheme due to false propaganda.*) It will not fit to be known as Tao if it is not laugh at. (*According to Gandhi, "First they ignore you, then they laugh at you, then they fight you, then you win." The truth is normally grasped by the minority while the majority simply pays no heed to find out the truth. People once thought the world was flat, that bathing was unhealthy, and that there was such a thing as the divine right of kings. Many things "everyone knows" just aren't so. The minds of the majority are preoccupied by the wrong concepts lobbied and deeply implanted by the interest group with self-interest. The people thought they are awake because the dream is so real, when they are plugged into "The Matrix" and receive the sweet-dream stimulant from "The Intelligent Mind". "Evil triumphs when good men do nothing". "There is, however, a limit at which forbearance ceases to be a virtue". "Toleration is good for all, or it is good for none".—Edmund Burke.*) Hence, there is a conventional wisdom which says that: the obvious way is often unnoticed; (*That is why many people often uttered the phrase "why didn't I thought of that?". What you see does not mean others will be able to see it.*) The way to go forward looks like

68

it is going backward; (*Increasing self-reliance is obviously the way forward but many choose to be looked after by the government with various social welfare schemes, ignoring the conventional wisdom of "no free lunch in the world", until it is too late to find out that they voluntarily participated in self-fooling game of "getting paid by paying somebody" and the country eventually goes bankrupt. Does anyone want to rely more on his parents as he grows older?*) Smooth way looks like it is uneven. (*Smooth way that is not absolutely smooth may be better than slippery smooth path. Making it smoother will increase the likelihood of accident.*) The best benevolence looks like no generosity is given; (*The best benevolence is needs no benevolence. When the society is peaceful and everyone feels happy to rely on himself, there is no need for generosity from anybody, much less the government. This is the best benevolence that the leader can give the people.*) The whitest cloth looks like it is contaminated; (*When it is absolutely white, every tiny little dust will become easily visible. We must not mistake the one without visible dust as the whitest because the grayish tone or texture overshadows the dust which is actually there. We must not reject a person just because he becomes imperfect when he made a little mistake. A good leader must not be afraid to make mistake or being imperfect.*) The widespread benevolence looks like not enough is done; (*A good leader must not do too much for the people so that it will become both necessary and rewarding for everyone to learn new skills and create values rather than a burden on the society. In this manner the benevolence reaches the widest extent but no one really feel that it has anything to do with the leader.*) The sturdy benevolence looks like the creator is lazy to make it perfect; (*It was actually purposely left imperfect. A good leader must be ready to ignore criticisms such as lazy, inefficient, etc.*) Naturally existed quality looks impure or tainted; (*Absolute purity is so artificial. The best diamond is one with impurity. Individuals pretending to be extremely religious are unnatural.*) The biggest square has no corner; (*When it is so big that no one ever reach the edge, no corner can be found. The most righteous person has no ego to scold or rebuke the behaviors of anyone, no sharp corner to poke no one.*) The biggest apparatus never will be completed; (*The universe is still expanding. It has unlimited functions, unlike any apparatus which can be identified as competent in certain aspects. A good leader must not endeavor to become an expert in certain areas but to have wide knowledge albeit not the depth. It is better to be the user rather than the apparatus.*) The best music does not need to be loud; (*The music from the Nature is the best music. The truth of Tao does not need screaming to prove its worth.*) The biggest appearance has no shape; (*The universe has no shape. The truth has no boundary. No one can describe what is absolutely right and what is absolutely wrong. If something is absolutely right or absolutely wrong, it needs no debate. The greatest humanity has no nationality. This is the truest sense of globalization.*) Tao is so far-reaching but it is not famous or well-known; (*Tao is all encompassing. It is not "A" and it is not "B". Any name given is just a tag for convenient sake. Because its boundary cannot be determined therefore Tao cannot be easily identified or named, it cannot become famous like simpler physical theories that produce Nobel Prize winners.*) Therefore, harmonizing with Tao is the only way to have good start and ends with good outcomes. (*Going against the free markets will always create more troubles than benefits in the long run. We must not just look at the short-term effects. Government intervention must not continue indefinitely.*)

Verse 41

反也者 道之动也 弱也者 道之用也 天下之物生于有 有生于无

Events happen in cycle are the exercises of Tao. (*History repeats itself, albeit not in the exact similarity. It does rhythm.*) Being weak is the working style of Tao. (*Practicing Tao may not yield fast results. Many good policies do not show good outcomes in the short term. Similarly, many bad policies do not show side effects in the short term.*) Everything in the world is given birth by something in existence. Existence is given birth by Nothingness. (*Logically, the root of everything cannot be "something". Otherwise, what gives birth to that "something"?*)

Verse 42

道生一 一生二 二生三 三生万物
万物负阴而抱阳 中气以为和 天下之所恶 唯孤 寡 不谷 而王公
以自名也
物或损之而益 益之而损 故人之所教 亦议而教人
故强梁者不得死 我将以为学父

Tao started as one indefinable thing. That one thing splits into two, the
Ying and Yang. (*Like electron and proton.*) Combination of Ying and Yang
produces the third thing. The third thing evolves into millions of things.
Everything has some Ying and some Yang. The right amount of both
Ying and Yang will produce harmony, giving rise to something. (*Different
amounts of Ying and Yang that are just right produce different things in
the world.*) The status disliked by everybody is "orphan", "widower" or
"unworthy". But the king and duke use these terms to address themselves.
(*This was intended to remind themselves to be humble.*) Many things need
to forgo something in order to bring about flourishing. (*Losing something
may not always be a bad thing. The reestablishment may lead to a better thing
due to the reorganization of Ying and Yang. We must not be afraid to give up
something in order to gain more valuable objective. We must not be afraid to
renounce old myths and relearn advanced knowledge for us to reach new height
in our life.*) Many things flourish but lead to decline. (*Gaining something
may not always be a good thing. Imperialism always leads to catastrophic
fall in the history. Domination will lead to retaliation. All things that gain
strength will eventually decay. All bubbles eventually burst. See Verse 30 and
36. Learning new trading tricks may gain short-term prosperity but followed
by bankruptcy due to excessive risk taking and unsustainable business model.
Many people think that they can become rich by trading stock certificates and
other financial papers. It leads to the oversupply of college graduates in the
financial sector. The real economic value created by stock market is so small
compared to the personal wealth accumulated by the stock traders who never
make any real tangible products. The consequence is the bubble of illusory
economic growth and transfer of wealth from real value creators (farmers,
miners, manufacturers, etc) to stock traders. The only reason the stock index*

goes up is that the financial world swallowed up your taxpayer dollars, and those of your kids and grandkids. Not because there's anything at all in the economy that's moving upwards. The bubble will eventually burst as it has happened many times in the history but the people don't seem to learn from those experiences. The young fools always claim "this time it's different" from that applied to the doddering old fools who lived years ago. Well, the difference is this time we're headed for the biggest crash in history. The poisonous debt will take many years to be repaid compounded by stubborn unemployment rate because the skills of many workers and some infrastructure will become useless after the bubble burst. "There is no means of avoiding the final collapse of a boom brought about by credit expansion. The alternative is only whether the crises should come sooner as the result of a voluntary abandonment of further credit expansion, or later as a final and total catastrophe of the currency system involved."—Ludwig Von Mises.) I received the teaching from the ancestors. I will discuss and teach the knowledge to others. The use of brute force will not lead to graceful ending. I will use this as the fundamental principle in learning of Tao. (*Use of soft power, take no confrontational stand, is advocated by Lao Zi. Quantitative Easing, a phony name for money printing out of "toxic assets", is a financial brute force to bail out the bankers from bankruptcy. The ramification will not be graceful. This monetary system prioritizes creditors and shareholders over labor, and it will eventually lead to political turmoil.)*

Verse 43

天下之至柔 驰骋于天下之至坚 无有入于无间 吾是以知无为之有益也
不言之教 无为之益 天下希能及之矣

The softest thing in the world runs freely around the hardest thing in the world. (*Wind flows everywhere it likes. Earth stays where it is. Being flexible can be invincible. Having no hard asset means maximum mobility. Having hard property and attach to it means being restrained and live with the prosperity as well as disaster coming its way, and the risk of losing what you have. Having a free and flexible mind means easy adaptation to any situation. Having fixated prior knowledge and virtuous values will bring*

72

more sufferings than happiness. One will risk falling prey to his own bias.) Nothingness can penetrate seamless body. (*Even seamless body cannot escape the effect of Tao. Perfect plan can fail if it goes against Tao.*) This is how I knew non-intervention is beneficial. (*Tao is everywhere. Going along with Tao is beneficial even if it causes some undesirable outcomes. Failure is not always bad. Failure leads to success. A man who dares to fail will dare to try more new things. Trying to play God and intervene unnecessarily, in the name of protecting the people you dearly care, may see some short-term benefits but suffer the long-term ramification. Nature will take its course if we give it a chance.*) The teaching by no instruction and the benefit of non-intervention are the best. There are few that can match them. (*Lead by example. Learning motivated by the need to learn is better than harangue from the teacher to listen to more lectures than necessary. No intervention creates the need to learn the necessary skills and create values. Expecting a helping hand will degrade the drive to work hard.*)

Verse 44

名与身孰亲 身与货孰多 得与亡孰病
甚爱必大费 多藏必厚亡 故知足不辱 知止不殆 可以长久

Glorious name and body, which is dearer? Body and wealth, which is more valuable? (*Glorious name and wealth will have no meaning if you never have a life. You have no life if you are just a tool or robot programmed such that you want to accomplish certain missions.*) Acquiring and losing (glorious name and wealth), which is more alarming? (*If you have something you value so much, you will be worrying of losing it. Why acquire it in the first place? If you are losing something you didn't have when you come to this world, you are just profiting less from this world. Why should you be alarmed? It is not wise to be over ambitious. It is not wise to be afraid of losing something.*) Loving something too much will incur big expenses. (*When you have obsession for something, you will waste a lot of money acquiring and maintaining it. When you love someone too much, you will waste a lot of time and emotion on unnecessary worrying and intervention.*) Accumulating too much will lead to big loss. (*Keeping more wealth is preparing it for thief to get rich quick by taking control of the wealth. It is not wise for leader to amass too much power.*) Therefore, being contented with life will avoid being insulted. Knowing when to stop will avoid getting into dangerous territory. This is the ingredient for longevity. (*Security in terms of social, economic and defence lies in the practice of not wanting too much and not stretching too far. Wanting too much will create depression in other parties and eventually backfire.*)

Verse 45

大成若缺 其用不弊 大盈若冲 其用不窘 大直如诎 大巧如拙 大赢如绌 躁胜寒 静胜炅 清静可以为天下正

The biggest achievement looks like it has imperfection. (*Perfection means there is no room for improvement. Hence, the natural progression will have to be degradation. In this sense, perfection is a form of imperfection. Achievement without imperfection means there were too much sacrifices and that is the biggest imperfection. Nothing is perfect in the universe. Even Tao is no exception. Imperfect man can never create perfect social and economic system.*) Being imperfect will have inexhaustible benefits. (*It is good to stay imperfect so that we do not start going downhill. Staying imperfect will provide a reason for other parties to feel less pressure.*) The fullest pot looks like it is empty. (*It is occupied by nothingness.*) The empty space has invaluable use. (*Being receptive of good and bad ideas as well as morality will have far reaching benefits.*) The long straight line looks like it is crooked. (*Natural things are all crooked. Even artificially straight line will look crooked when it is long enough. It is a matter of viewpoint. No individual is absolutely straight. So, no one is in the position to make himself the benchmark for others to follow. Even if you are straight, you will still look crooked by some people, but you don't have to feel alarmed.*) The biggest trick looks like it is clumsy. (*Pretending to be foolish will make others unsuspecting. Pretending to do no intervention is the biggest trick to make the people resolve their problems themselves and not relying on the government. The outcomes will be better than pretending to be clever at intervening. The universe is extremely tricky that many events are unpredictable but some scientists thought that they can explain all the phenomena using scientific laws and theories. By the way, scientists figure out those laws and theories all by themselves through observations and deep thinking. Didn't they?)* The biggest win looks like it is losing. (*The leader seems to lose the opportunity to accumulate power and wealth when he doesn't control the people and collect little tax from the people. However, the resulting social and economic growth will make the country stronger and the government revenue increased. It will be the biggest win for the leader.)* Exercising the body can overcome chilling cold weather. Keeping calm can overcome hot weather. (*The people know what to do or how to adapt to the changing environment. They don't need the government to tell them what to do. Central planning is unnecessary.)* Staying calm and no intervention will bring equilibrium to the world. (*Intervention will distort the system. The reaction of the system will be larger when there are more interventions. The higher is the peak of the boom, the lower is the valley of the bust. In statistics, this kind of phenomenon is known as regression toward the mean. A good leader should stay neutral and not try to disturb the free-market system too much.)*

Verse 46

天下有道 却走马以粪 天下无道 戎马生于郊
罪莫大于可欲 祸莫大于不知足 咎莫憯于欲得 故知足之足 恒足
矣

When the world is peaceful, horses can be used in farming operations. When the world is in chaos, war horses will live in the remote war zones. (*It is so wrong to argue that war can contribute to economic revival or growth due to demand and investment in weapons and military supplies. The incorrect use of resources leads to tremendous waste and destruction. The winning force may gain from robbing the properties of the rivals but the gain is always much smaller compared to the sum of wealth destruction. War hawks are just considering their potential gains and totally disregard the losses of other nations. It is so unethically selfish.)* The greatest sin is no greater than greedy for unlimited benefit. The greatest crisis is no greater than not contented with life. (*Desire for unlimited prosperity and happiness will lead one into taking on unnecessary risks and wasting one's life pursuing things that do not matter in life.*) The greatest trouble is no worst than desire to obtain ambitious success and wealth. Therefore, the satisfaction of contented with life is the real satisfaction.

(We will live a life of abundance, in our own perception or definition of abundance, when we are contented with what we make and what we have, no matter how our neighbors look at us. We must not draw our portrait by looking at another person but the mirror. Those who are not contented with their lives, irrespective of whether they are wealthy or not, will use every available opportunity to take advantage of others. These individuals are poor, either financially or mentally. "If we command our wealth, we shall be rich and free; if our wealth commands us, we are poor indeed."—Edmund Burke. If our brains have been conditioned to think that we cannot live without this and that, we perceive non-essential things as basic needs, we are not free and we will not be happy. If we have never experience hunger, any annoyance beyond that in term of living standard is trivial and we are more fortunate than perhaps more than half the population of the world. We must be grateful with what we have instead of focusing on what we lack. In the developed world, the older generation have committed the sin of living beyond their means and spent the money they shouldn't have gotten. They were able to enjoy their life to the fullest and continue business as usual without improving the productivity because the economy was surviving on government stimulus coming from raising national debts and government guaranteed liabilities. They created the economic crisis which makes the younger generation suffer the scarcity of jobs compounded by the burden of paying off the debts. The richest ten percent controlling more than half the total wealth is also causing social instability and riots because capitalists have been allowed to become wealthy at the expense of their friends or neighbors. The crisis is not in the best interest of everybody, including the rich. The empire dream gets them into trouble and continued to torture them. Harassment and provocation of other countries leads to retaliation, causing trouble to national security and the need for big military spending to sustain the vicious cycle. Anti-U.S. sentiment continues to increase and amplify the Islamic extremist dimension of the U.S.-led War on Terror. All these are due to ungratefulness; wanting high living standard with little labor and wanting

perpetual peace by suppressing the "potential threats". Anyway, gratitude is not for the mentally lethargic. Gratitude requires emotional intelligence and it takes mental toughness and discipline. Compared with those who dwell on daily hassles, people who give thanks exercise more regularly, complain of fewer annoyance, feel better about their lives overall. They also feel more loving, forgiving, joyful, enthusiastic, and optimistic about their futures, while their family and friends report that they seem happier and are more pleasant to be around. However, insincere giving of thanks will not escape the eyes of the receivers. And being grateful (to Mother-nature) with what we have doesn't mean we shall do nothing to improve our lives or prevent squalid politicians from taking away our liberty and the future of our children. Politicians should be grateful to the people who pay for their salaries, and not the other way around. Politicians should be grateful to be able to live in peace and not abuse the power given by the people and destroy the country.)

Verse 47

不出于户 以知天下 不窥于牖 以知天道 其出也弥远 其知也弥少
是以圣人不行而知 不见而明 弗为而成

Without having to go out of the house, it is possible to know the state of affairs of the world. (*It is impossible to know every details of the world. It is even harder to get first-hand information from ground-truth measurements by the leader himself. No leader ever relies on complete information to make a decision because the required response cannot wait. By looking at the macro data and trends, with an in-depth understanding of history and Tao, a good leader shall be able to take the appropriate actions.*) Without having to peek out at the window, it is possible to know how the Nature evolves. (*The four seasons evolve in a predictable cycle. Although there will be some differences every year, the general patterns do not change. The same applies to many social and economic issues in the world. By applying the fundamental principles, one will be able to predict the general direction of the evolution. There can be changes in no-change; there can be no-change in changes. Everything changes with time but there is always some patterns or trends that do not change. One needs to keep in mind this Law of Nature in the decision making process.*)

One who goes further will know lesser. (*When one is too ambitious to know too many details, or too many theories from different experts with conflicting views, he will become bewildered if he cannot find the middle ground. In this sense, his real knowledge is getting lesser.*) Therefore, great leader does not need to travel to every corner of every village to know what is happening in the country. He does not need to see with his own eyes to understand the real situation. He does not intervene to achieve any pre-determined objective and the country will achieve the deserving status by itself. (*A good leader should learn from the Mother-nature; do what he ought to, is able, willing and ready to do; with no pre-determined objective or ambitious expectation; no ambitious of benefiting each and every people equally as long as the statistical results are reasonable; let the free markets function by itself. In the upbringing of children, we don't have to hold their hands all the time; don't have to see each of them scores 'A' in every subject; don't expect every one will be equally successful; have faith in the Nature that each of them will find their destiny. When we have faith, we have hope. When we have no faith, we have no hope. When we have faith that most workers will try to produce excellent work if they are given the right environment, we will not be in denial of the shortcomings but enthusiastically try to create the right environment. There is a chance our efforts will bear fruits. When we have no faith in them, we will instead try to set new rules and scrutinizing methods to "whip the dying horse" stronger and expect it to get up and start running again. Even if the plan works, the dying horse may start walking but it will not be able to run. There is no hope of business growth and it would be better to liquidate the business than to continue the agony.*)

Verse 48

为学者日益 为道者日损 损之有损 以至于无为 无为而无不为
将欲取天下也 恒无事 及其有事也 又不足以取天下矣

Studying is to gain increasing knowledge. Practicing Tao is to weaken the desire. Keep weakening the desire until there is no more desire to intervene or carry out ambitious plan. No intervention and no problem are unresolved. (*Non-intervention is the strategy; big achievement is the final objective. Non-intervention means believes in the free market system, have faith in the people and allow the people to excel with their own effort. Big achievement can be obtained when everyone thinks and acts as dignified individual who is responsible for his own life and decisions. In the transition from developing country to developed country, government interventions must be decreased with time, not increased, until no intervention is needed eventually. Modern-days children are taken care of too much by their parents and become less independent and less resilient as opposed to the original intention of making them competitive against their peers. The results are worst when the paranoid central planning is wrong, making the children lack of certain aspects of personality such as moral, ethics, interpersonal skills, emotional stability, ability to make judgment and organize values into priorities, etc. Some children were spoiled into becoming drug and computer-game addicts.)* To be respected by the world, great leader will do nothing to meddle around. *(Nobody likes to be interfered. Good leaders are admired for protecting the freedom of the people, not for meddling in the household matters of the people or in other countries. A good leader should be like the sun; there are places with too much sunlight and places with too little sunlight, but everybody respects the sun although it stays still and does not meddle around.)* If he starts to meddle around, he will not have enough strength to capture the trust of the world. *(Meddling will create more problems in the course of solving problem that does not exist. Vicious cycle will start to set in. The chaos will become beyond the capability of anyone to resolve.)*

Verse 49

圣人恒无心 以百姓之心为心 善者善之 不善者亦善之 德善也
信者信之 不信者亦信之 德信也
圣人之在天下 歙歙焉 为天下浑心 百姓皆属其耳冂焉 圣人皆孩
之

Great leader has no personal wish. He will always put the interest of the people at his heart. He will treat courteous individuals courteously. He will also treat rude individuals courteously. In that way he will cultivate the people to be courteous. *(People who fight fire with fire usually end up with ashes. Forgiveness does not change the past, but it does enlarge the future.*) He will treat trustworthy individuals with trustworthy deed. He will also treat untrustworthy individuals with trustworthy deed. (*A good leader will always keep his promises, whether or not the other party did the same.*) In that way he will cultivate the people to be trustworthy. Great leader should lead the world with no greed/ego/obsession. In that way he will cultivate the people of the world to be ingenuous. The people will naturally keep their ears and eyes on the leader and apply their cleverness or pseudo-intellectual. Great leader will always show them a gracious look, treat them like his children, and keep educating them to be ingenuous.

Verse 50

出生 入死 生之徒十有三 死之徒十有三 而民生生 动皆之死地
之十有三 夫何故也 以其生生之厚也
盖闻善执生者 陵行不辟兕虎 入军不被甲兵 兕无所揣其角 虎无
所措其蚤 兵无所容其刃 夫何故也 以其无死地焉

People are born to life and eventually set out into death. The young and vibrant constitutes 3 out of 10 people. The old and dying constitutes 3 out of 10 people. Those who desire to live longer but their actions lead them to premature death constitute 3 out of 10 people. What is the reason? It is because they have too much desire to live longer. (*Some people work too hard to accumulate wealth so as to sustain longer retirement in the future but discovered at the point of death that they had never lived. Some people chase prosperity but make too many enemies and got killed or persecuted. Some people eat too much and too nutritious wishing to live longer but discovered that they contracted all kinds of rare illnesses that do not happen to middle-class people. The US is paranoid about their national security despite having the most number of advanced defense technology. They want to have no security threat but their actions of provoking numerous nations in the world lead to retaliation in the form of terrorist attacks. The US should stop sticking its nose into other nations' business and start being a good neighbor. Many people want to be loved but instead, due to ego, their behaviors are such which pushes love away and engage in mutual hurt. It is irony but that is what happened in many cases.*) I heard that individuals who are good at taking care of their lives will not have to avoid rhino and tiger when they walk on the forested hill; they will not get hurt in the mid of a war. Rhino has no chance to use its horn; tiger has no chance to use its claws; weapon has no chance to use its knife-edge. What is the reason? It is because they never enter into fatal situation. (*The safest way to live is to have no enemy. The best way to survive is to keep away from danger.*)

Verse 51

道生之 而德畜之 物刑之 而器成之 是以万物尊道而贵德
道之尊 德之贵也 大莫之爵而恒自然也
道生之 畜之 长之 遂之 亭之 毒之 养之 覆之 生而弗有也 为
而弗恃也 长而弗宰也 此之谓玄德

Tao created all things. Benevolence nurtures them. Different things take different shapes. Different apparatus are formed. (*Different things have different functions and usefulness.*) Therefore, all things respect Tao and pay high regard to Benevolence. Tao is respected and Benevolence is highly regarded because they do not dictate compliance to any specific requirement but allow all things to evolve naturally. Tao created all things and nurtures them; grows and enriches them; leads them to maturity and let them fall ill; cultivates them but also let them die naturally. It doesn't own or possess them. It cares for all things but doesn't expect anything in return. It raises them but not controlling them. This kindness is called the Great Benevolence. (*A good leader should care for the people but never assume he has the right or responsibility to impose his morality on the people for any political objectives.*)

Verse 52

天下有始 以为天下母 既得其母 以知其子 既知其子 复守其母
没身不殆
塞其兑 闭其门 终身不堇 启其兑 济其事 终身不棘

The world has a common beginning. It is the mother which produces everything in this world. If we understand the root source, we will be able to explain the reasons that give rise to the various things. (*If we understand the fundamental laws, we will be able to explain the various physical phenomena due to the natural functioning of those physical laws. For example, we know gravity causes apple to fall towards the ground. We can use the same gravitational law to explain the orbits of planets and asteroids.*) If we know the reasons of various things and return to hold strong belief in the root source, we can avoid any danger till the end of our life. (*We must not forget Tao or the fundamental laws and do something stupid when we are overwhelmed by the happenings around us. The lack of faith in Tao can have serious ramification.*) Block the loophole and close the door, and there will be no hardship for the whole life. (*No whistling sound from the flute and no shortcut passage. Close the mouth and don't use too much cleverness. Unwarranted cleverness or pseudo-intellectual will cause trouble.*) Open up loophole for quick fix will leave us no respite for the whole life.

见小曰明 守柔曰强 用其光 复归其明 毋遗身殃 是谓袭常

Being able to spot fine details is having clear vision. Being able to persist in practicing soft-skills is the real strength. Apply the wisdom of Tao and return to consider the careful observation of the circumstances will leave no peril to our body. This is the long handed down common sense. (*Don't follow hard rules in doing things but be flexible to make any necessary adaptation to the circumstances with close observation. Common sense is not so common these days.*)

Verse 53

使我介然有知也 行于大道 唯施是畏
大道甚夷 民甚好解
朝甚除 田甚芜 仓甚虚 服文采 带利剑 厌食而财货有余 是谓盗
夸 盗夸 非道也

When I had a little knowledge and walked on the Great Way, I was worried of stepping into the evil way by mistake. The Great Way is quite smooth, but many people like to use winding small roads and shortcuts. The palace is lavishly built, but the farmland is overgrown with weeds; the storehouse has little reserve. The king wears beautiful clothes; carry luxurious swords; throw oversupplied food into waste and accumulate excessive wealth. This is the behaviour of the thug leader. Being a thug leader is not the correct Way of life. (*Like giant stock traders, thug leader also create employment to help him accumulate excessive wealth but no real tangible product is ever made. They don't amount to increased production for the whole economy. Furthermore, they suck away the wealth of real value creators (farmers, miners, manufacturers, etc) like parasites. What good does those employment make for the economy? Hooligans create fear in the society and then pretend to be the protectors who collect fees to provide security. Stock investment companies work in complicity with bankers to multiply money supply in the economy to enrich themselves at the detriment of real value creators who see their savings diluted by newly printed money every day. They then offer wealth management services that promise to make the savings work harder to beat the inflation by investing in stocks. They have simply created the problem so that they can market their solution.*)

Verse 54

善建者不拔 善抱者不脱 子孙以祭祀不绝
修之身 其德乃真 修之家 其德有余 修之乡 其德乃长 修之国
其德乃夆 修之于天下 其德乃博
以身观身 以家观家 以乡观乡 以邦观邦 以天下观天下 吾何以
知天下然兹 以此

A good builder will build irremovable building. (*It will be irremovable when it has a strong foundation. It will be even more irremovable when no one wants to remove it. A civilization will be long lasting when it is built on strong foundation and it does not offend any external forces.*) A good enfolder will not loosen his arm. (*No force is needed when the person wants to be enfolded or no one wants to force open the arm. Alliance is welcomed when mutual trust is built and mutual interest is guaranteed. No citizen will abandon his country if his self-interest is tied to the country. The system must provide a sense of ownership to the citizens, not just a sense of belonging. They must really*

feel they have a stake in the country. Harangue for patriotism is unnecessary.)
If the descendants follow this practice, the worship to ancestors will not
discontinue generation after generation. Practicing it in self improvement
will bring real benevolence to oneself. Practicing it in the family will
bring spare benevolence. Practicing it in the village will bring long-lasting
benevolence. Practicing it in the state will bring bountiful benevolence.
Practicing it in the world will bring widespread benevolence. (*Everyone
needs to govern his body, family, organization, if not the country. The correct
Way of life will bring peace and prosperity.*) Watch over yourself for own
interest; watch over your family as a member of the family; watch over your
village as a member of the village; watch over your state as a member of
the state; watch over the world as a member of the world. (*Keep a personal
interest in observing the things and events around us. Tao is everywhere. It can
be learnt from everything. All happenings follow certain fundamental laws.
These laws are applicable in micro as well as macro levels. By applying them in
understanding the behaviors of individuals, families, villages and states, it is
possible to understand the behaviors of the world. Not forgetting that you are a
member of the family will remind you not to overlook the interest of the family
in the face of attractive interest to your selfish desire. By considering yourself as
a global citizen, you will not be overwhelmed by the interest of the state and
overlook the interest of the world. We are all interconnected. What happens to
the world will also affect us.*) How do I know the natural progression of the
world? It is with this logic.

Verse 55

含德之厚者 比于赤子 蜂虿虺蛇弗蛰 攫鸟猛兽弗搏 骨弱筋柔而
握固 未知牝牡之会而朘怒 精之至也 终日号而不嗄 和之至也
知和曰常 知常曰明 益生曰祥 心使气曰强 物壮则老 谓之不道
不道蚤已

A person with profound benevolence standing has a pure heart like a
baby. (*He is seen not a threat to anything.*) Hornet, scorpion and snake will
not sting him. Ferocious bird and animal will not attack him. (*Legend
has it that Romulus, the reputed founder and first ruler of Rome, and his*

twin brother Remus, were orphans suckled and raised by a she-wolf.) His bone is weak and his muscle is soft but his grip is firm. (*He does not seem offensive but he is firm and fearless.*) Like a baby who has no knowledge of sexual attraction but yet the baby can have penile erection. It is due to the vast intrinsic energy in the body. Baby can cry the whole day and his sound does not become hoarse. (*When righteous becomes firmly built in one's heart, he will naturally have the energy to do what is right.*) It is due to perfect harmony with Tao. Agreeing to harmonize with Tao is a natural rule or natural thing to do. Accepting the natural rule is wise. Desire to live beyond the limit will bring disastrous consequences. Letting your feeling dictates your energy in emotional reaction is acting in undue confidence of one's strength. All things that gain strength will eventually become weaken. (*Nothing can gain strength indefinitely. Strong wind does not blow the whole day; and rainstorm does not last for a few days. Why is it so? Even the Nature cannot keep up the force for too long. How much less so the capability of man?—Verse 24*) Thirst to gain strength does not harmonize with Tao. Not harmonizing with Tao will lead to perish.

Verse 56

知者弗言 言者弗知
塞其兑 闭其门 和其光 同其尘 挫其锐 解其纷 是谓玄同
故 不可得而亲 不可得而疏 不可得而利 亦不可得而害 不可得
而贵 亦不可得而贱 故为天下贵

A wise leader who really knows Tao will not dictate the conduct of others. A person who assumes he knows everything and tries to prescribe a standard way of life for everyone is not wise and doesn't really know Tao. (*Be accommodative because the way we prefer may not be the right way for others. Don't try to teach the people what to do in each and every matter but let them learn on their own, follow their heart and intuition to find what they truly want to become. Individual who talks a lot on what are the right and wrong ways often do not really know what he is talking about. Zhao Gua was familiar with the literature on arts of war and often win in debates over his father Zhao Sher, who was a legendary army general of Zhao State during the*

Warring States Period. However, Zhao Sher knew his son was familiar only with the theory but not the real mastering of the arts of war. In his will, he reminded the king of Zhao State never to appoint his son as an army general. However, the king was deceived by the enemy and ignored the advice of Zhao Sher. In the war against the Qin State's army, all 400,000 soldiers led by Zhao Gua were slaughtered or buried alive by the enemy.) Block the loophole and close the door. *(No whistling sound from the flute and no shortcut passage. Close the mouth and don't use too much cleverness or pseudo-intellectuals.)* Light reflection becomes soft and not sparkling. *(Don't outshine others. Display no difference from the majority.)* Dust settles into place. *(Live in harmony with others and don't stir up conflicts. Stability is more important than everything else.)* Sharp edges become smooth. *(No sharp edges to poke no one.)* Chaos is resolved. *(Tolerate and compromise.)* This is the best equalization. Therefore, a wise leader will not be particularly beloved *(he doesn't try to please anybody)*; not particularly distanced *(nobody hate him)*; not expected to give out benefits *(he doesn't act as if he is a cash cow or power center who can bend the rules. Billionaire political investor will not pour money into politics if the government will not give him subsidies, provide him monopoly privileges, or the ability to erect all types of barriers against his competitors, or something "worth" spending the big bucks on)*; not feared of to cause any harm *(he doesn't appear to be violent and no one wants to harm him either)*; not accepting any honorary title from anyone *(he doesn't need honorary title or formal recognition ceremony)*; and leave no misconduct to be disrespected by anyone. *(A wise leader will live in harmony with others.)* He will then be respected by the world.

Verse 57

以正治邦 以奇用兵 以无事取天下
吾何以知其然哉
夫天下多忌讳 而民弥贫 人多利器 而国家滋昏 民多伎能 而奇
物滋起 法物滋彰 盗贼多有

Apply righteous *(straight measures that harmonize with Tao)* in ruling the country. Apply innovativeness in manoeuvring the army in battle against enemy. (*Cleverness can be used to defend the country against external enemy but not in ruling the country.*) Apply no intervention (*no busy-body in domestic issues of foreign countries*) to gain respect of the world. How do I know these are the prudent ways? It is from the following observations: when there are many forbidden rules in the world, the people will be poor. (*When the people are not free to make things for a living due to regulatory bureaucracy or religious myths, the free-market system is not fully embraced, the economy cannot prosper. When there are too many psychological burdens and the people's minds are constrained by norms and rituals, the people cannot be innovative to make necessary adjustments or learn new skills to adapt to changes in the surrounding, social-and economic-wise. There are "opportunity costs" involved, not just the costs of doing business in cash term, but in terms of the innovation and growth we don't have because of government policies, laws, and regulations.*) When the people keep sharp weapons to protect themselves, the society will become increasingly chaotic. (*When the notorious are not punished, the people will feel the need to keep sharp weapons and guns to protect themselves. When justice is not served and bullying is rewarding, more people will resort to violence. In the wake of a sluggish economy and uncertainty about the upcoming election, Americans are buying guns and ammo by the truck load. The National Shooting Sports Foundation (NSSF) said at its annual trade show that strong sales in 2012 may surpass the record-setting 2011. It is a vicious cycle. More weapons will lead to more crimes, followed by even more weapons acquired by the people.*) When the people are encouraged to be skilful and inventive, strange things will be created. (*A lot of strange products in the markets are unnecessary. Cleverness or pseudo-intellectual is undesirable as opposed to real wisdom.*) When the laws become complex and comprehensive, bigger thugs and thieves will emerge. (*People are inherently clever. When the laws try to out-clever the people, it encourages the people to be more innovative to defeat the laws. Rule of laws is good, but villains and fraudulent businessmen have learnt to conceal evidence and are brave to challenge the laws, and get away with insufficient evidence to prosecute them. They know how to use crooked ways to counter the straight rules. Is the rule of law trustworthy if petty offences are prosecuted while multimillions frauds defeat the prosecutor and smile all the way to the bank? Whenever there is a comprehensive law, there will always be a lawyer smart enough to get around it. It is easy to put the blame on the prosecutor and the police, but the problems will remain. Is it possible to have enough laws or comprehensive laws to ensure zero crime? Is the problem due to a lack of laws? Let the judges do the judging instead of the lifeless book of laws. "It is not what a lawyer tells me I may do; but what humanity, reason, and justice tell me I ought to do." "All human laws are, properly speaking, only declaratory; they have no power over the substance of original justice." "Bad laws are the worst sort of tyranny." "People crushed by law, have no hopes but from power. If laws are their enemies, they will be enemies to laws; and those who have much to hope and nothing to lose, will always be dangerous."—Edmund Burke)*

是以圣人之言曰 我无为也 而民自化 我好静 而民自正 我无事 而民自富 我欲无欲 而民自朴

Hence, the wisdom from great leaders in the past says: I have no ambition to fix everything therefore the people will resolve their problems themselves and become peace loving. (*People will avoid conflicts when they know the government will not help them to resolve the conflicts. When Wang Yang Ming of Ming Dynasty became the magistrate of a town where there were many lawsuits, he declared that he would not handle anymore cases and he educated the people to be tolerant and care for each other. The town became peaceful within a short period of time.*) I like to keep quiet therefore the people will rely on themselves to find the right ways. (*Free-markets will make it necessary and rewarding to adjust oneself to the right ways to get what he wants, wealth as well as social justice. Of course, there will be no free-markets when there are superpowers, dominant corporations or power centres, which are able to control and manipulate the markets.*) I do no intervention therefore the people will become rich by their own efforts. (*In the book "An Inquiry into the Nature and Causes of the Wealth of Nations", Adam Smith says: "Every individual necessarily labours to render the annual revenue of the society as great as he can. He generally neither intends to promote the public interest, nor knows how much he is promoting it . . . He intends only his own gain, and he is in this, as in many other cases, led by an invisible hand to promote an end which was no part of his intention. Nor is it always the worse for society that it was no part of his intention. By pursuing his own interest he frequently promotes that of the society more effectually than when he really intends to promote it. I have never known much good done by those who affected to trade for the public good.")* I desire to have no desire therefore the people will become ingenuous. (*Inflated development is not good for society. Due to the desire of the leader to boost development, corruption is often extenuated. It leads to establishment of dominant corporations and power centres which destroy the free-markets for the benefit of the "selected race". The GDP figure is not necessarily representative of the well-being of the general public. Wealth inequality and social injustice is not in the best interest of everybody. The rich think that they can enjoy what they steal from the public and use the wealth to protect themselves. However, all will be gone with the wind when the tipping point is reached. It is sad to see many people being misled into a belief of great fallacy that corruption is necessary for development to take place. The obvious is overlooked. Greater development can be achieved when there is no corruption because the potential of the whole population including millions of brilliant minds is maximized, and the progress will be on a firmer footing.*)

Verse 58

其政闷闷 其民屯屯 其正察察 其邦缺缺
祸 福之所倚 福 祸之所伏 孰知其极
其无正也 正复为奇 善复为妖 人之悉也 其日闯久矣 是以方而
不割 廉而不刺 直而不绁 光而不眺

When the government is lacklustre (*not ambitious and does not pretend to be clever*), the people will be ingenuous. When the government is clever (*having intelligence to dig every details*), the nation will be cunning (*to out-clever the government*). Misfortune always piggybacks with fortune. (*Everything has its flipside. Certain rules may be good to have but they are not without bad repercussion, and certain regulations may be advantageous to one group of people but not for others.*) Fortune always piggybacks with misfortune. (*Everything has its flipside. Failure in regulating something may seem undesirable but it may lead to a greater success. When the society is tolerant and forgiving, the people will be capable of loving others. Trying to play God and intervene unnecessarily, in the name of protecting the people you dearly care, may see some short-term benefit but suffer the long-term ramification. If a society needs strict laws to maintain its order, it shows that the people have low civic spirit that they will tend to be sneaky whenever the law enforcement is absent.)* Nobody knows how good or how bad it can get. There is no standard on how much regulation is just right. The right can turn into unjust innovativeness. *(Smart lawyers can turn the interpretation of the laws against the innocent victims for the benefit of their perpetrator clients. Only the rich don't become broke hiring smart lawyers to represent them. Are the laws always good to have?)* The good can turn into evil. *(Tax on the rich to subsidize the poor may be seen as a virtue or a "necessary evil". However, it may become an "unnecessary evil" when it incentivize the poor to do nothing to improve themselves and continue to be burden of the society, dependent upon generosity, and be cemented to the bottom as poor people.)* The bewilderments of the people have existed for too long. Hence, great leader is righteous but has no ego to criticize the behaviors of anyone *(no sharp corner to poke no one)*; honest but has no ego to impose his morality on anyone; frank but doesn't behave anarchistic *(having the right argument doesn't give one the rights to wildly disrespect others)*; bright but not frightening *(not outshining, belittling or suppressing others from voicing their opinions)*.

Verse 59

治人 事天 莫若嗇
夫唯嗇 是以早服 早服是谓重积德 重积德则无不克 无不克则莫知其极 莫知其极 可以有国 有国之母 可以长久 是谓深根固柢 长生久视之道也

In governing the people and dealing with the nature, there is nothing more important than being thrifty. By being thrifty, one can conserve the resources, in terms of material as well as affection, and make early preparation to face future challenges. *(Resources are limited. Politicians want to do too many things only to fail doing anything right. Overspending by raising government debt and guaranteed liabilities will lead to bankruptcy and the ramifications will be felt on the day of reckoning.*) Having early preparation means emphasize accumulation of benevolence. (*Encouraging the people to rely on themselves is leading them to become versatile and having the capability to make the most out of limited resources. This is the best benevolence that the government can do for the people.*) Emphasize accumulation of benevolence will make no threat invincible. No threat invincible means no limit on the achievable level. No limit on the achievable level means the country can be preserved. (*The society will be peaceful and the people are capable of protecting the country against any external force.*) When the country has a strong foundation, longevity of the nation will be secured. This is the Way to build a country with deep rooted sturdy foundation, and give it a long life and durable existence. (*"The most valuable economic substance in the world is capital. It is not "money" if we define money as pieces of green paper. Governments cannot create wealth by printing money. If they could we wouldn't have to work. The formation of capital plus a culture of entrepreneurship is the only way to create economic well being. When government policies destroy capital it diminishes everyone's economic well being. Capital is saved wealth. If you produce goods and you make a profit and save the profit, then you have created capital; ditto with your labour. If you spend all of your wages, you've saved none of the wealth created from the goods you made and you have no capital."—Jeff Harding writes in an article entitled The Economics of Mass Destruction.*)

Verse 60

治大国若烹小鲜
以道莅天下 其鬼不神 非其鬼不神也 其神不伤人也 非其神不伤
人也 圣人亦弗伤也 夫两不相伤 故德交归焉

Governing a big country should be like cooking a small fish. (*We must not use intense high flame and stir the fish frequently. On the contrary, the small fish should be left in the hot cooking oil on low flame to fry it slowly until golden brown.*) Applying Tao in governing the world, evil tricks will not become accepted belief or practices. (*Many are misled into a belief of great fallacy that capitalism is all about making profit and there is nothing immoral in cheating the clients for own profit. Capitalists have been allowed to become wealthy at the expense of their friends or neighbors. Many capitalists use Initial Public Offering (IPO) as the exit strategy of their business; use inflated accounting figures to deceive investors into paying more than the real worth of the companies with no sincere intention to continue the business growth after the IPO to reward the investors. The business founders take profit and sometimes even siphon the real business to new private companies for personal gains and abandon the public listed ones. There is no intention of ensuring a win-win provision and mutual trust between the investors and the management. Hence, to avoid being fooled by the unethical capitalists or overcame by greed for huge return of being an "angel investor", one important investment rule of Warren Buffett is never to consider a company unless it's been around for 10 years or more and can demonstrate a record of consistent performance. Nevertheless, capitalism is actually about giving the people total freedom and incentives to produce, save, invest and behave prudently. According to Adam Smith, markets' ability to self-regulate, to ensure maximum efficiency and to grow can somehow be threatened by monopolies, tax preferences, lobbying groups, and other "privileges" extended to certain members of the economy. Privileged groups using the government machinery (in the forms of favorable monetary policies, regulations to make smaller players unable to compete or barriers against entry of new players, preferential government spending and guarantees, etc.) or using market dominations to manipulate prices to "steal" from the public must be condemned as unacceptable corrupt practices. "Among a people generally corrupt liberty cannot long exist". "Whenever a separation is made between liberty and justice, neither, in my opinion, is safe".—Edmund Burke)* Not only the evil will not become god, the existence of the fallacy will not harm other people. Not only the fallacy will not harm other people, the Sage also will not harm anybody or disapprove the belief. *(When Tao is upheld, nobody can use the bible to impose certain moralities on others. The Sage need not stop the religious belief. The Sage need not force anybody to follow his teachings. Diversity should always be celebrated. The concept of religion is similar to beautiful lies; as in lies with "just cause". If you can accept beautiful lies and believe that you need to use them to achieve certain objectives, then religious belief is good for you. If you are of the opinion that any lie is unacceptable, and you have the conviction to tell no lie, then you must never impose any religious belief on others.)* Because both the Sage and the fallacy do not harm anybody, therefore the benevolence of each can interplay and contribute to the same logical conclusion. (*Nothingness and Existence exist together, given different names but they are both part of Tao. When the world adopt a common standard for beautiful, that is ugly. See Verse 2. Beautiful and ugly shall be accommodated and neither shall be eliminated. The logical conclusions of ethical self-interest and concern for others are actually the same. Selfishness and altruism can be opposite and yet parallel. See Verse 13. Bad people can serve as reflections or negative examples to good people. See Verse 27. The existence of threats will make it necessary and rewarding for the people to stay alert, ever ready to face challenges, and not become complacent with current status or rely on the government to look after them. False impression of zero threat will lead to insurmountable threat due to zero capability to handle even a small threat. Trying to eliminate all threats is unwise. There are different types of bacteria and fungal in our bodies. They are harmless when there is a delicate balance between them and the body has sufficient immunity against them. However, if we use certain antibiotic or antifungal soap to disturb the balance unnecessarily, one group of microbe may be killed but another group may use the opportunity to mutate or proliferate and becomes a threat beyond the immunity level of our bodies. Therefore, we should instead leave them alone to live in harmony with our bodies and only regulate when a group of microbe is showing sign of proliferation. Similarly, a government should respond to the community, not try to anticipate or lead it.*)

Verse 61

大邦者 下流也 天下之牝 天下之交也

牝恒以静胜牡 为其静也 故大邦以下小邦 则取小国 小邦以下大邦 则取于大邦

故 或下以取 或下而取 故 大邦者不过欲兼畜人 小邦者不过欲入事人 夫皆得其欲 则大者宜为下

Big country shall behave like the downstream of a river (*receptive of all small rivers from the upstream*). It shall act as the womb of the world (*nurturing*

93

all things, helping everybody wherever possible), and the centre for people of the world to meet and build diplomatic relations. Feminine behavior (*soft, tolerance, and calm*) is quiet but it is always better than masculine behavior (*hard-line, tough, and energetic*). It is because of its quietness. (*Being quiet and no meddling around will gain the trust of everybody as opposed to fear. Being quiet will conserve energy as opposed to restless moves that will exhaust one's energy.*) Therefore, a big country which is humble in dealing with a small country will gain the trust of the small country. (*Using military power to inflict fear and gain alliance is not prudent. Fear tactic will only produce short-term affiliation.*) Small country which behaves humbly in dealing with big country will gain the acceptance of the big country. Hence, the government shall either be humble to gain trust or be humble to gain acceptance. (*Being humble doesn't make one loses anything other than not feeding one's ego. On the contrary, narcissistic and masculine behaviour give no benefits at all. When one really has the strength of the male, he doesn't need to behave masculine to gain the respect of others. See Verse 28.*) A big country wants nothing more than the affiliation of small countries. (*Belittling a small country may lead to unforeseeable consequences when it forms alliance with the enemy.*) A small country wants nothing more than the acceptance and protection from a big country. Each will get what they want. (*It is a win-win for everybody.*) A big country needs to be especially humble. (*Empires gain strength, become bloated, and finally collapse on their own blunders. This is a natural phenomenon which happens repeatedly in history. See Verse 36. The leader of a big country should learn the lessons to give the country a long life and durable existence. The British sold opium to the Chinese, took their gold and silver, and robbed their antiques. The decay of the Qing Dynasty was accelerated. The Chinese were awakened that they needed to rely on themselves in order to defend their dignity; a forgotten wisdom from the ancestors. Amid the growing economic strength of China as well as some Commonwealth countries, do the British expect any gratitude from the former colonies of Great Britain? Animal eats the fruits from the plant, shits on the ground, and the plant benefited from the fertilizer. Does the plant need to be grateful to the animal?*)

Verse 62

道者 万物之注也 善人之宝也 不善人之所保也

美言可以市 尊行可以贺人

人之不善 何弃之有 故立天子 置三卿 虽有拱之璧以先驷马 不
若坐进此道

古之所以贵此道者何也 不谓求以得 有罪以免与 故为天下贵

Tao is an attention of all things. Good individuals treat it as treasure. Even bad individuals want to preserve and make use of it. (*Small robber cannot become big thug leader if he doesn't make use of Tao.*) Noteworthy words can gain adoption. Respectable deeds can gain admiration. However, things that people do not like shall not be discarded. (*Things that are not commonly thought as worthy may not necessarily be worthless. The obvious way is often unnoticed. What you see does not mean others will be able to see it. See Verse 40.*) Being crowned as the king or promoted as the highest minister may be offered precious jade and luxurious four-horse-drawn carriage in the ceremony. However, it is not better than simply offered this Tao. (*Ceremony and being celebrated is unnecessary. Tao is more precious than anything. Good things need not necessarily be adored by everybody.*) Why did the ancestors treasure this Tao? Isn't it because they can get what they want out of their enterprise, or avoid penalty due to their effective prevention? Therefore, Tao is treasured by the world. (*Sciences help people get what they want and avoid what they don't want. Therefore, Sciences are treasured by the people. It is not because it is a religion or something. Many people have chosen the wrong thing to treasure, such as power and money. It leads to unhappiness to all parties, and gives rise to all kinds of undesirable things, including corruption. Power is not precious if it comes with great responsibility. Money is not precious if it comes with great worry of losing it, to robbers or family members, or government-financial-complex through dilution of buying power. Private capital can be destroyed or stolen by government-financial-complex using all kinds of squalid methods, in the disguise of providing social welfare. It is all paid by the people. It doesn't mean we didn't pay just because we didn't see the money physically taken out of our pockets. It is like magic. Where else can the money come from? It is definitely not from the politicians!*)

Verse 63

为无为 事无事 味无味 大小 多少 报怨以德
图难乎其易也 为大乎其细也 天下之难作于易 天下之大作于细
是以圣人终不为大 故能成其大
夫轻诺必寡信 多易必多难 是以圣人犹难之 故终于无难

Pursue no ambitious objective, do no intervention, and aspire for no feeling of success or pleasure, whether it is big or small; much or little. (*Have no ambition to achieve glory. Do ordinary work and do not meddle around. Never seek for feeling of success or fun of doing something. Do whatever needs to be done but never seek for perfection. Do not assume our doing for just cause is absolutely right because there is a chance that we are heading in the wrong direction but we are overconfident to overlook the obvious. It will be too late when we press the gas too much and reach a point of no return. A good leader should not set any target but step aside and let the people do what is necessary to benefit themselves and the country by the way. Don't try to be clever. The people are always cleverer than the leader. Otherwise, the country will have no bright future when everybody relies on the leader to show them the ways. As F.A. Hayek famously argued in The Road to Serfdom that people of higher intelligence have different tastes and views, so they never want to get on top in politics. "He had no failings which were not owing to a noble cause; to an ardent, generous, perhaps an immoderate passion for fame; a passion which is the instinct of all great souls". "I have never yet seen any plan which has not been mended by the observations of those who were much inferior in understanding to the person who took the lead in the business."—Edmund Burke*) Repay betrayal or hatred with benevolence. (*War breeds war, peace breeds prosperity.*) To attempt difficult problem, start with the easy parts. To pursue big issue, start from the small parts. (*In dealing with difficult problem, we have to start somewhere and, very often, we cannot attempt to take on the toughest culprit when we are not yet ready in terms of power and resources. To achieve long-term results, we cannot be short-sighted and treat only the symptoms.*) The difficult target in the world can only be achieved by doing easier tasks one at a time. The big target in the world can only be achieved by eyeing small targets one at a time. (*A newly liberated country cannot expect to become a developed country overnight. Overambitious will result in no progress or worst situation. Lessons must be learnt from the attempts of Middle Eastern rulers to modernize their states to compete more effectively with the European powers in the late 19th and early 20th centuries. In all the cases, the money to pay for the reforms was borrowed from the west, and the crippling debt this entailed led to bankruptcy and even greater western domination. Additionally, westernisation created professional armies, led by officers who were both willing and able to seize power for themselves, and caused a bigger problem that has plagued the Middle East ever since. The recent declaration by Foreign Minister Yang Jiechi that "China will remain a developing country in the coming decade" is a wise move. We do not become able to bear more responsibilities just because we or others say we can. Chasing artificial title will end up facing real tragedy. This is one of the famous words of wisdom from Cao Cao in the history of the Three Kingdoms.)* Great leader will never aim to achieve big ambition; therefore, he can become the leader who presided over the big achievement. (*Not ambitious is the strategy; big achievement is the objective.*) One who makes promises lightly will seldom be able to keep his words. (*"Hypocrisy can afford to be magnificent in its promises, for never intending to go beyond promise, it costs nothing."—Edmund Burke*) One who presumes all problems are easy to solve will face a lot of difficulties. (*Politicians who promise fast and painless solutions to current debt crises and security issues are not trustworthy. Ben Bernanke, the US Federal Reserve Chairman, said in 2002: "The U.S. government has a technology, called a printing press, that allows it to produce as many U.S. dollars as it wishes at no cost." He referred to a statement made by Milton Friedman about using a "helicopter drop" of money into the economy to fight deflation. He has since been referred to as "Helicopter Ben". The world have subsequently faced with many financial crises, due to his ignorance of the warning signs and denying there was a housing bubble, but used his oversimplified money-printing method to postpone the economic collapse. Evidences have shown that his grand experiments with the economy using unconventional measures do not work.*) Therefore, great leader will always view a problem as difficult (*so that he doesn't overlook any aspects, including the repercussions and possible traps*). Hence, he will end up with no difficult problem unresolved. (*Complete solution is formulated and problem is resolved part by part, little by little, as opposed to a big hoo-hah at the onset but end up with bigger problems that are insurmountable. In the face of current debt crisis, businessmen called for the government to keep loosening the credit control, claiming that businesses will go bankrupt otherwise. Public servants picket over government austerity drives to cut deficit, claiming that they cannot survive without government generosity. University students demand the government to absorb their study loans and provide free tertiary education, in the name of cultivating the "national assets". Everybody sees the government as the benevolent nanny without realising they are entrusting their lives in the hand of the "big bad wolf" who disguises as the loving grandmother. Loose credit control has given rise to too much money being printed electronically and leads to credit bubbles that have started to burst one by one. Continue loosening of credit control will feed the blood-sucking businessmen at the expense of the general public because of the resulting high inflation. The difficulty of the people to own a house or buy enough food for their families is not because of the unavailability of credit. The real cause of the problem is dilution of buying power due to too much fiat money flooding the markets. The GDP numbers are inflated or sustained by Central Banks' money printing and money multiplication effect of Fractional Reserve Banking System. The GDP numbers are fuelled by public and private debts; it is not a representation of the real tangible products output. For example, lesser number of machineries produced can contribute to the same GDP numbers due to price increase; even less number of machineries will be sold if there was no easy credit to encourage spending, fuelling artificial demand, and the GDP numbers will drop further. Government does not make any products which amounts to economic growth. More government officers only lead to more bureaucracy which is detriment to the economy. When a big percentage of GDP is contributed by government spending, it only means the government has sucked away the fund required for healthy operation of the free-market. It fuels unnecessary consumption or wastage of resources to keep the economy going in terms of the GDP numbers as opposed to real improvement of productivity. The "benevolence" of providing more government jobs to the people is actually setting up the whole nation to face a more devastating economic collapse in the future. It would have been better if the people had been allowed to face their hardship as a motivation to find real jobs or become entrepreneurs that produce real products. Government guaranteed study loan is created to benefit the higher education industry more than the noble excuse of helping university students. Many students have been deceived to get a degree which doesn't land them a job or improve their productivity but instead make them bear a debt burden as "national service" to the economy. It is again a case of fueling unnecessary demand for useless products. Can a country afford to provide unlimited number of tertiary education places for free? Is it really necessary? Will it benefit all the people or it only gives special privileges to some who rip the benefits without the qualms of claiming they benefit the country in the future while in actual fact the scheme only contributes to the self-benefit of the scholarship recipients? Who will actually pay for it and will they get their share of returns on investments? If a student really thinks that a university degree will give him a better life, he should take a loan and invest in his education rather than expecting the public to pay for it. A country will have a bleak future if everybody wants to use the government as a machine to mine personal benefits and doesn't care where the money comes from. "Since the State began to control education, its evident tendency has been more and more to act in such a manner as to promote repression and hindrance of education, rather than the true development of the individual. Its tendency has been for compulsion, for enforced equality at the lowest level, for the watering down of the subject and even the abandonment of all formal teaching, for the inculcation of obedience to the State and to the "group," rather than the development of self-independence, for the deprecation of intellectual subjects."—Murray N. Rothbard, an eminent educationist and professor in economics, argues in his book "Education: Free and Compulsory".)*

Verse 64

其安也 易持也 其未兆也 易谋也 其脆易判 其微易散
为之于其未有 治之于其未乱 合抱之木 作于毫末 九成之台 起
于蔂土 百仞之高 始于足下 为之者败之 执者失之
是以圣人无为也 故无败也 无执也 故无失也
民之从事也 恒于几成而败之 慎终若始 则无败事矣 是以圣人欲
不欲 而不贵难得之货 学不学 而复众人之所过 能辅万物之自然
而弗敢为

When the condition is calm, the social order is easy to maintain. When the symptom is not obvious, it is easy to formulate the cure. When the problem is weak, it is easy to resolve. When the problem is small, it is easy to dissipate. Take prevention before problem arises. Regulate before chaos erupts. (*Irving Fisher wrote in the late 1930s, after observing the Great Depression and the actions of the Federal Reserve, noted that the best and only way to deal with a credit bubble was to prevent it from happening. Once they develop, there is no easy, painless way back. Good banking is produced not by good laws but by good bankers.*) Big tree trunk grows from tiny shoot. A nine-storey tower is built up from ground level on a small piece of land. Climbing up a high mountain of thousands feet has to start from the first step. Those who try to do thing by brute-force will fail, and those who are too stubborn will lose the grasp of the situation. Great leader will do no ambitious work and therefore no failure. (*Non-ambitious works are easy to be successfully completed. Non-ambitious works do not necessarily mean insignificant tasks. As Sun Zi said, "What the ancients called a clever fighter is one who not only wins, but excels in winning with ease. Hence his victories bring him neither reputation for wisdom nor credit for courage. He wins his battles by making no mistakes. Making no mistakes is what establishes the certainty of victory, for it means conquering an enemy that is already defeated". "The good fighters of old first put themselves beyond the possibility of defeat, and then waited for an opportunity of defeating the enemy. To secure ourselves against defeat lies in our own hands, but the opportunity of defeating the enemy is provided by the enemy himself. Thus the good fighter is able to secure himself against defeat, but cannot be certain of defeating the enemy. Hence the saying:*

One may KNOW how to conquer without being able to DO it.") He is not stubbornly loyal to his own doctrine therefore he doesn't lose the chance to succeed. When the people pursue certain projects, they often reach the point of near success but end in failure. We must pay enough attention towards the end like what we did at the beginning. Then we will have no possibility of failure. Therefore great leader desires to have no desire, and no obsession for rare objects. (*No desire to have quick win but progress at a strong footing. No desire to win a hundred battles but to win a war. A war cannot be won overnight but a battle must be ended quickly in order to conserve energy and resources. A battle can be ended quickly by means of conquering an enemy that is already defeated. Rare objects, including success, do not matter in life. We do not bring them into our grave. Conversely, we look stupid to be obedient to the dogma of certain interest groups.*) Learn to have not learnt; and reverse (*not to repeat*) the mistakes of others. (*Learn everything but never assume we have learnt everything about something. Be cautious to make no mistakes, and be ready to hear the views and opinions of others. Learn for the fun of learning and never set any ambitious target to achieve. The good outcomes will come naturally.*) Have the ability to assist all things in enhancing their natural life but dare not intervene. (*Confucius said: "Do not impose on others what you yourself do not desire". However, imposing on others what you desire is undesirable. The legs of duck are short, but we are not supposed to make them longer. The legs of crane are long, but we are not supposed to make them shorter. We may love exquisite wine but offering it to our animal guests is not entertaining to them. It is better to leave the people alone to live their natural life. Don't try to be clever and intervene unnecessarily.*)

Verse 65
故曰 为道者非以明民也 将以愚之也
民之难治也 以其知也 故以知知邦 邦之贼也 以不知知邦 邦之
德也 恒知此两者亦稽式也
恒知稽式 此谓玄德 玄德深矣 远矣 与物反矣 乃至大顺

Therefore, it is said that the leader who practices Tao aims not to be known as a clever guy by the people. On the contrary, the objective is to be perceived as a foolish man. (*The greatest intelligence looks foolish.*) The people are difficult to rule because they are inherently clever. Therefore, applying cleverness to rule the country is being the culprit of the country. (*When the leader is clever and opportunistic, he educates and encourages the people to out-clever against him and be even more opportunistic. Just as the leader thought that he is innovative in cheating the people, with all kind of "benevolent" packages such as social welfare and Medicare, some people are even more innovative in cheating the leader to gain personal benefit and let the leader takes the blame. It is better to pretend to be foolish so that the bankers and big corporations will leave him alone because he is "useless" to them and they will have to go back to play by the free-market rules.*) Using simple and unsophisticated ways to rule the country is providing the real benevolence to the country. Knowing these two different methods is the key to mastering the fundamental technique to rule the country. (*Use cleverness as discretional as possible but always pretend to be foolish.*) Mastering the fundamental technique leads to the great benevolence. The great benevolence is deep and far reaching. It follows the cycle of how all things behave and finally leads to the greatest harmony with the Nature.

Verse 66

江海之所以能为百谷王者　以其善下之也　故能为百谷王
是以圣人之欲上民也　必以其言下之　其欲先民也　必以其身后之
故居前而民弗害也　居上而民弗重也　天下乐推而弗厌也　非以其
无诤与　故天下莫能与争

The river and the sea can become the kings of hundred streams because they take the lower position. Hence, they can receive the water from the hundred streams and become big river and sea. Therefore, great leader who wishes to keep a higher position than the people must be humble with his words. If he wishes to lead the people, he must take the back stage. (*Let the people take the front stage and contribute their mental and physical energies. Give them the full credits as opposed to claiming that the success is contributed by the leadership role. Liu Bang declared publicly that he was no better than his helpers in all aspects in the struggle to topple the Qin*

Dynasty and fight against Xiang Yu. Yet no one could take over his position as the leader and eventually the first emperor of the Han Dynasty.) Hence, the people are not afraid of him being the leader. The people do not feel any weight with him being on top. The whole world is happy to support him and not dislike him. This is because he does not compete with anyone. (*He is already the leader. He doesn't need any promotion and there is no higher position for him to be promoted to. He does not need to take away the credits of the people.*) Therefore, nobody in the world can compete with him. (*He doesn't compete with anyone on who is more brilliant therefore no one can compete with him. See Verse 23.*)

Verse 67

小邦 寡民 使有什佰人之器而毋川 使民重死而远徙 有车舟无所乘之 有甲兵无所陈之 使民复结绳而川之 甘其食 美其服 乐其俗 安其居 邻邦相望 鸡犬之声相闻 民至老死不相往来

In ruling a small country with small population, even though military organization is available, it is best to have no need to use it. When the people are afraid to die in a war and emigrate to far away land, even if military trucks and boats are available, there won't be anyone to ride them; even if shields and blades are available, there is no place to display them. The preferred ruling is to tie the self-interest of the people to the country so that they will stay (*to protect their families and properties*). Allow the people to build an environment where they can enjoy delicious foods, wear beautiful clothes, integrate happily with the culture, and live peacefully in their houses. Neighbors are able to watch each other; the sound of chickens and dogs from the neighbors can be heard; the residences grow old and die but never need any help from their neighbors. (*People live in a community neighborhood and not alone in the jungle because they feel the needs for mutual help when they are in trouble. It comes with the implied obligation to help and not just receive help from the neighbors. However, it will be no fun to live in a chaotic community where the neighbors need help on a daily basis. It is best that everybody can live a life of abundance, therefore need no assistance from anyone. The people are as free as fish living in the river without having to help each other.*)

Verse 68

信言不美 美言不信 知者不博 博者不知 善者不多 多者不善
圣人无积 既以为人 己愈有 既以予人 己愈多
故 天之道 利而不害 人之道 为而弗争

Trustworthy words are not flowery; flowery words are not trustworthy. (*"Flattery corrupts both the receiver and the giver."—Edmund Burke*) Individuals with deep knowledge do not have wide knowledge; individuals with wide knowledge do not have deep knowledge. Virtuous individuals do not have much asset; rich individuals do not have much virtuous values. Great leader does not accumulate asset. He puts all his energy into helping the people but it makes him more abundant. (*The country becomes wealthier therefore the leader will have more spare resources, not only in terms of material but also spiritual support of the people.*) He gives generously to the people but it makes him wealthier. (*Higher GDP can be achieved with investment in public infrastructure. A good boss rewards his employees the right way and higher productivity makes him richer.*) Therefore, the Tao of the Nature is it benefits and does not harm all things in the world. The Tao of the human is to do good to everybody and does not compete with them for anything. (*A good leader does whatever he can to help the people but sets no ambitious target to achieve. Every success will come to him naturally.*)

Verse 69

天下皆谓我大 大而不肖 夫唯不肖 故能大 若肖 久矣其细也夫
我恒有三宝 持而保之 一曰慈 二曰俭 三曰不敢为天下先
慈 故能勇 俭 故能广 不敢为天下先 故能成事长 今舍其慈 且
勇 舍其俭 且广 舍其后 且先 则必死矣 夫慈 以战则胜 以守则
固 天将健之 如以慈垣之

Many people in the world say that I have great philosophy but inconsistent with any common wisdom. Because it is inconsistent with common wisdom therefore it can become great philosophy. If it is common knowledge, it would have long become insignificant. (*Unity of the minds is advocated by the interest groups so that the people can be easily controlled. Common wisdom may not always be the correct way as we have been educated to believe it as the truth. We must aggressively challenge the conventional wisdom. The biggest appearance has no shape. If the philosophy is simple enough that even common people can accept it, there will be nothing great about it.*) I have three precious principles that I uphold with determination; the first is unconditional love for others (*no expectation of any return*); the second is thrifty, emotionally and financially (*exercise moderation; resources are limited, so are affections; don't offer affection or assume everybody wants our affection*); the third is dare not take the lead in the world. (*Live a simple life. Lie low and not to portray oneself as the best person in the world who know everything about everything. This is opposed to narcissism which assumes oneself is always right and the whole world must follow his ways.*) One who has unconditional love will able to be courageous. (*Parents love their children unconditionally therefore they are courageous to sacrifice even their lives to protect their children.*) One who is thrifty will be able to reach out more widely. One who dares not take the lead in the world will be able to lead the accomplishment of various tasks. (*Champions always face challenges from competitors therefore they are always busy handling those challenges and are not able to accomplish more important jobs. President always faces more attacks than his deputies.*) If we abandon unconditional love but only behave courageously; abandon thrifty but still try to reach out widely; abandon compromise and stay behind but be the first to charge forward or fight for leadership role; we will face great danger. (*"All government, indeed every human benefit and enjoyment, every virtue, and every prudent act, is founded on compromise and barter."—Edmund Burke*) A leader with unconditional love for his people will be able to win when he goes to a battle; have a sturdy defense against aggressors when he set up a defensive wall. (*Leader with personal political ambition will not gain full support from the people. "I venture to say no war can be long carried on against the will of the people."—Edmund Burke*) When the Nature wants to fortify something, it will use unconditional love to preserve it. (*If a leader really wants to protect his country, he must sincerely love his people.*)

Verse 70

善为士者不武 善战者不怒 善胜敌者弗与 善用人者为之下 是谓
不诤之德 是谓用人 是谓肥天 古之极也

Good military officers are not enthusiastic to go to war. (*They only go to war when there is really no other option. They do not show off their masculine might.*) Good commanders of military troops will not get angry easily. (*Sun Zi said: "If your opponent is of choleric temper, seek to irritate him. Pretend to be weak, that he may grow arrogant." "A king must not initiate a war because he is enraged; a commander must not start a battle because he is resentful. For while an angered man may again be happy, and a resentful man may again be pleased, a state that has perished cannot be restored, nor can the dead be brought back to life."*) Good military generals who are good at winning a war will not engage the enemies. (*Sun Zi said: "Hence to fight and conquer in all your battles is not supreme excellence; supreme excellence consists in breaking the enemy's resistance without fighting."*) A leader who is good at recruiting helpers will behave humbly to listen to their opinions and ideas. These are known as the benevolence of not competing (*Win by not competing head-to-head.*); known as caring for human's lives (*Sun Tzu said: "In the practical art of war, the best thing of all is to take the enemy's country whole and intact; to shatter and destroy it is not so good. So, too, it is better to recapture an army entire than to destroy it, to capture a regiment, a detachment or a company entire than to destroy them."*); known as enriching the Nature. (*The Nature loves all things, living as well as non-living things. Minimizing destruction is harmonizing with the Law of Nature.*) These are the best principles of the ancient time.

Verse 71

用兵有言曰 吾不敢为主而为客 吾不进寸而退尺 是谓行无行 攘
无臂 执无兵 乃无敌矣
祸莫大于无敌 无敌近亡吾葆矣 故抗兵相若 则哀者胜矣

The ancient art of war said: I dare not be the aggressor but the defender; I don't step one inch into the land of other country but retreat a few feet away from our border. (*Retreat can be designed to entice the enemy, to unbalance him, and to create a situation favorable for a decisive counter-stroke. The retreat is, paradoxically, offensive.*) Because I hide in a secret recess, the enemy wants to mobilize his troops but do not know where to mobilize (*This tactic is adopted perfectly by Mao Ze Dong and his generals in the war to liberalize China and in the Korean War.*); the enemy wants to swing his arms but find that he is liken to no arm; the enemy wants to use his weapon but find that he is liken to no weapon to use; thence I am invincible. (*Sun Zi said: "The general who is skilled in defence hides in the most secret recesses of the earth; he who is skilled in attack flashes forth from the topmost heights of heaven."*) However, the greatest danger is no greater than presume invincible. (*We can hide but we cannot run. We have to face the enemy eventually. Every preparation, including tactical attack and reconnaissance supports, needs to be made carefully to defend ourselves. Sun Zi said: "To secure ourselves against defeat lies in our own hands, but the opportunity of defeating the enemy is provided by the enemy himself."*) Presume invincible means one is not far from losing everything. Hence, when both opposing troops have comparable strength, the side which is being invaded and made to fight against the aggressors will win. (*The spirit to protect their families and properties will give them the determination and perseverance to deter the enemy. The side which is not arrogant but fighting for the noble reason of defending their compatriots and belongings will have the moral high ground and will power to fight as compared to the aggressors who are trying to besiege the city of other country. Of course, the defender can still lose the war if the people do not have a sense of ownership of the country and they feel as though they are unworthy souls sent to the warzone to die for the ruler; or the defender is lacking in defense technology and skills. According to Sun Zi, war is always about economic gain rather than moral. Currency war is the latest game of the governments in the world today. As much as one country wishes to embrace free-markets economy, it must defend the people against the "evils" of Keynesianism practiced by foreign countries. Isolationism is not an option. Knowledge of defense techniques in currency war is vital.)*

Verse 72

吾言甚易知也　甚易行也　而人莫之能知也　而莫之能行也
言有君　事有宗　其唯无知也　是以不我知　知者希　则我贵矣　是以
圣人被褐而怀玉

What I advocated is easy to understand the logic and easy to put into action. However, few want to understand and apply it. (*It is so easy to understand the fact that when everybody becomes rich, no one will be left out or become poor. When the pie becomes bigger, everybody will get a fair share big enough to avoid starvation. However, everybody refuses to understand the fact and instead wants to amass benefits for himself. Everybody wants to stuff his stomach with bigger share of the pie than he really needs. What is the reason? Everybody wants to win, amass more benefits than his neighbors "before it is too late". Athletes take steroids to win the titles they don't deserve and yet talk about sportsmanship in the public. There is a lack of faith in collective prosperity. And religious beliefs have lost their credibility and ability to harangue the people to have no greed when people become cleverer and not succumbed to the lies of some religious leaders who have motives of achieving personal political objectives. Political ambitions destroy religions. It is better to make the people more knowledgeable and embrace ethical self-interest where individuals will enjoy self-interest of being loved by loving others; love Mother-earth so that She is able to love us. "Education is the cheap defense of nations."—Edmund Burke*) What I said has its basis and its historical fact. Because one doesn't know the theoretical basis and the historical fact, therefore he cannot understand my ideology. Because there are few who understand my ideology, therefore I become distinctive (*not because the ideology is difficult to understand*). Great leader doesn't mind to wear simple cloth but kept beautiful jade inside. (*A good leader doesn't mind to look ingenuous but possesses real wisdom.*)

Verse 73
知不知 尚矣 不知不知 病矣 是以圣人之不病 以其病病也 是以
不病

Knowing one doesn't know everything is wise. Not knowing what needs to be known is imprudent. (*Nobody knows everything about everything. One is wise to admit insufficient knowledge of certain matters as opposed to one who is in denial. Not knowing there are matters that one doesn't know means there will be no quest to find out the truth. Even if we know certain intellectual subjects, we need to aggressively challenge the conventional wisdom; seek out genuinely different ways of looking at things and perspectives that challenge what we may have accepted as being the truth for decades. We need to be flexible and rethink what we know.*) Great leader will not become imprudent because he dislikes becoming imprudent. Therefore he is not imprudent. (*A good leader is wise to recognize imperfection as imperfection and doesn't try to hide the fact or sweep the problem under the carpet. He will instead seek to find out the truth and avoid the use of wrong governing ideology and enter into a vicious cycle of endless interventions.*)

Verse 74
民之不畏畏 则大畏将至矣
毋闸其所居 毋猒其所生
夫唯弗猒 是以不厌 是以圣人自知而不自见也 自爱而不自贵也
故去彼取此

If the people are tired of being frightened, then enormous frightening event will happen. (*At the end of Shang Dynasty in 1046 BC, the people were completely frightened by the King's tyrannous laws, cruel punishment methods, and human sacrifice as offering to gods. Eventually, the King's army and his equipped slaves betrayed him at the battle field by joining the rebels led by Zhou State to topple the Shang Dynasty, and denounced the gods. From that time onwards, the Chinese people in general do not believe in gods anymore. "Gods ruling over life and death" is the belief system invented in the early civilizations when people seek to understand the world in order to make it a slightly less scary place. Continuing the belief system means not progressing from early civilization. Laws enacted based on religious beliefs or rituals are undesirable. "People crushed by law, have no hopes but from power. If laws are their enemies, they will be enemies to laws; and those who have much to hope and nothing to lose, will always be dangerous."—Edmund Burke)* Government must not displace the people from their land; do not interrupt the people's way of living. *(The people must be allowed to make anything for a living without government bureaucracy and heavy tax.)* Because the government does not interrupt the people, it will not be disliked. Therefore, great leader seeks to have wide knowledge but never assume his view is always correct; self-satisfy but never assume he has a higher status. *(A good leader who wishes to be on top of the people must be humble with his words. See Verse 66.)*

Verse 75

勇于敢者则杀 勇于不敢者则活 此两者 或利或害 天之所恶 孰知其故
天之道 不战而善胜 不言而善应 不召而自来 单而善谋 天网恢恢 疏而不失

Those who have the courage to dare defying Tao will get killed. Those who have the courage to dare not defying Tao will live. These two types of courage, one will bring benefit while the other will bring detriment. The things that the Nature hates, nobody knows what are the reasons. *(The earth orbits around the sun. It is what it is. Nobody can expect the sun will ever orbit around the earth instead. Although everything in the world changes every day, there are certain patterns or rules-of-change that do not change. Defying the rules-of-change or Ways of harmonizing with the Nature will be detrimental no matter how courageous we are.)* The Laws which the Nature follows are: never fight with anyone but always be good at winning; *(Sun Zi said: "Hence to fight and conquer in all your battles is not supreme excellence; supreme excellence consists in breaking the enemy's resistance without fighting.")* never have to say a word but always good at responding; (*The Nature leaves all things to do whatever they like but it will reward or punish them accordingly.*) never need to be called upon but always come as it wishes; (*The Nature rains whenever and wherever it wants; it doesn't take order from anybody.*) simple but good at planning. (*The coming and going of four seasons are simple but they are well planned and never fail to meet the schedule. Just as some people thought they have found the way to defeat the Law of Nature, they always found out later that the Nature has quietly devised a plan to counter the cleverness of the people.*) The net of the Nature is extraordinarily wide; there are many loopholes but it never fails to capture anything. (*Nothing can escape the enforcement of Tao.*)

Verse 76

若民恒且不畏死 奈何以死惧之
若民恒且畏死 而为畸者吾将得而杀之 大孰敢矣
若民恒且必畏死 则恒有司杀者
夫代司杀者杀 是代大匠斫也 夫代大匠斫者 稀有不伤其手矣

If the people are not afraid to die anymore, what is the use of scaring them with death sentence? If the people are still afraid to die, and I catch and kill the criminals, who else dare to break the laws? (*Unfortunately, in today's world, there are people who love money more than their lives. They assume money can help them defy the laws. They are right so far until the rule of the rule-of-law is transformed, if that happens at all.*) So long as the people are afraid to die, (*People are afraid to die if they love to live. People may hate to live when they lose something more important than their lives, such as basic dignity and ability to protect their families.*) government will need to have official hangmen to execute the death sentence. Those who acted on behalf of the official hangmen to kill are like chopping a tree on behalf of a professional chopper. Part-time replacement chopper seldom does not hurt his hands. (*Law enforcement must be effective such that the people do not feel the need to take the laws into their own hands. Crime don't stop if people believe they can get away with it, irrespective of how severe is the penalty.*)

Verse 77

民之饥也 以其上食税之多也 是以饥
百姓之不治也 以其上之有以为也 是以不治
民之轻死也 以其求生之厚也 是以轻死
夫唯无以生为者 是贤贵生

The people are hungry because the king demands heavy tax; therefore they face hunger. The society is not peaceful because the king is ambitious to implement various programs (*such as using up resources to compete with neighboring countries, spreading "greedism" ideology as capitalism and resulting in wide income inequality, etc.*); therefore the society is not orderly. Many people are paranoid about death (*especially the well-to-do group*) because they are too ambitious to live longer (*their action lead them to premature death as mentioned in Verse 50*); therefore they are fearful to face the prospect of death. One who doesn't focus too much on longevity is wise in living a meaningful life.

Verse 78

人之生也柔弱 其死也亘坚强 万物草木之生也柔脆 其死也枯槁
故曰 坚强者 死之徒也 柔弱微细者 生之徒也
是以兵强则不胜 木强则折 强大居下 柔弱细微居上

Living humans are soft and weak. When we die, our bodies finally become stiff. All living plants are soft and crispy. When they die, they become rigid and degrading. Hence, it is said that the stiff belong to the group of death; (*Those who are not flexible are not far from death.*) the soft and fine belong to the group of lively. Therefore, using military might to threaten others will not win a war. (*Military strength can win a hundred battles but not a war; retaliation or infighting for domination will follow. The regime will fall either way.*) Wood which grows strong will break. (*Hard tree will be felled by strong wind or the chopper.*) Strong and big is lowly desired. (*It is not a good thing to become a threat to others. China is feared by the world when it becomes strong. Provocations start to pour in and it is not in everyone's best interest to have a war. China must stay soft and humble to prevent itself from being seen as a threat. Behaving hard only serves to satisfy temporary egoistic urge and no long-term peace. During Emperor Taizong's reign in the early Tang Dynasty, China were the largest and the strongest nation in the world. Although his army was able to defeat any enemies, he always preferred to pacify the aggressors to diffuse the threat at the borders. He adopted munificent policies to treat recaptured minorities, gained their respect, and was cherished as the Heaven Khan. Countries around the world seek to become coalitions of Tang. Chang'an became a world metropolis attracting travelers and businessmen from all nations. The Tang Dynasty do not only received foreign immigrants; they also received groups of foreign students to China to learn advanced culture. Among them were hundreds of Japanese students who studied at public expense.)* Soft and fine is highly regarded. (*The greatest courage looks cowardice. A good leader never shows off his courage but gives in on small issues so that he can conserve his energy to resolve big issues.*)

Verse 79

天之道 犹张弓者也 高者印之 下者举之 有余者损之 不足者补之

故 天之道 损有余而益不足 人之道则不然 损不足而奉有余
孰能有余而有以取奉于天者乎 唯有道者乎
是以圣人为而不恃 功成而不居也 若此 其不欲见贤也

The Way of the Nature that one should follow is like pulling the bow. If the aim is too high, lower it down. If the aim is too low, raise it. If the bow is pulled too hard, lighten the force. If the bow is pulled not enough, increase the force. (*Do not aim too high or too low. Too much force is as undesirable as too little force.*) Hence, the Way of the Nature is it trims the abundant and supplements the insufficient. (*In the nature system, anything which reaches the peak will start to decay, while another which reaches the bottom will have the chance to start growing. Inequality cannot go on forever. The collapse can be delayed if the growth of inequality is slow. No cleverness can beat the Law of Nature. Self-restraint and be contented with life is better than requiring someone to play God in socializing the wealth.*) The way humans behave today is the opposite. They cause detriments to the insufficient to benefit the abundant. (*The modern financial system encourages consumption by enticing the public with cheap credits to enrich the rich at the detriments of the poor. Even if the poor do not take any loan, they cannot escape the looting because inflation due to money printing dilutes the purchasing power of their salary. On the other hand, the government collect heavy tax from the people to enrich the financial-military-industrial-government complex using lies wrapped in noble causes or virtuous excuses.*) Who can have abundance and receive benefit from the Nature? (*Only the Nature can provide everything that we need. Entrepreneurs should use innovations and productivity improvement to gain prosperity instead of cheating the public, irrespective of whether the trick is legal or illegal.*) Perhaps only those who understand Tao can do it. Therefore, great leader does what is necessary to care for the people but doesn't expect anything in return. (*A good leader does not need to take anything from the people. He gets what he needs from the Nature. He does not accumulate asset. He puts all his energy into helping the people but it makes him more abundant. He gives generously to the people but it makes him wealthier. See Verse 68.*) He will not claim any credit for any success. In this manner, he does not wish to be known as a clever person. (*Give all the credits to the people. Good leader gives guidance by articulating the objectives he wants achieved and not direct instructions on how to achieve them. The greatest credit should be given to those who render the hardest work.*)

Verse 80

天下莫柔弱于水 而攻坚强者莫之能先也 以其无以易之也
水之胜刚也 弱之胜强也 天下莫弗知也 而莫之能行也 故圣人言
云曰 受邦之垢 是谓社稷之主 受邦之不祥 是为天下之王 正言
若反

In the world there is nothing softer and weaker than water. However, when it comes to attacking the hard and strong, there is nothing more superior to water. It is because water is indestructible. (*Water has no shape;*

therefore, it is not breakable, unlike rigid body which is considered destroyed when its shape is deformed. On the other hand, water is able to weaken steel and concrete structures. Tsunami can devastate a city. Sun Zi said: "Military tactics are liken to water; for water in its natural course runs away from high places and hastens downwards. So in war, the way is to avoid what is strong and to strike at what is weak. Water shapes its course according to the nature of the ground over which it flows; the soldier works out his victory in relation to the foe whom he is facing.") Soft like water can be more superior to rigidity. Weak can be better than strong. (*Being strong and arrogant to even dare to fight against the force of Nature will surely end up with dilapidation. Darwin's Theory of Evolution or Natural Selection is not synonymous to "survival of the fittest" suggested by Herbert Spencer. Survival is best guaranteed by running away from danger in the struggle for life. In this sense, the "fittest" is not the one that presumes it to be strong enough to defeat everything, or in the best physical shape, but the one that is ready to adapt and live in harmony with the environment. Big trees are felled by hurricane but not the grass.*) Nobody in the world doesn't know this fact; but few can endeavor to practice the ideology. There is a reason why great leader said "one who is receptive of unworthy things of the country can become the head of the society; one who is ready to face unfortunate events of the country can become the king." (*The king addresses himself as "orphan", "widower" or "unworthy" as a display of not undervalueing the position of the lower ranks. See Verse 39.*) The truth and correct way sometime looks opposite to common knowledge or mainstream teaching. (*Mainstream teaching is controlled by the interest group to inculcate obedience to the State and to the "group," rather than the development of self-independence. We must unlearn, do deep thinking, and relearn the truth and the correct way. It is hard to change a lifetime of looking at things in the way that we have been educated to believe is the correct way. But change is coming upon us all, and we either adapt or we pay the consequences. Acts of kindness and doing good are no doubt constructive for the best interests of everybody; nobody wants to live in an environment where the people are hostile to each other. Most of the teachings of Confucius are for world peace and human good until it is politicized by the emperors to "unite the people," make them obedient and never deprecate the wrong doings of the government.*

115

Acts of kindness can only be voluntary and people will embrace it if they really understand what it means to their wellbeing. Having the "just cause" doesn't give anyone the rights or responsibility to impose his morality or value system on the people. It only destroys the credibility of the "good intentions" because of the inherent political objectives. Can a military regime or hegemony control the people and the world forever? Are the people stupid enough to remain under iron-fist control forever? Is it in the best interests of the country and the world that the people are generally stupid and only the selected groups are educated to serve the dictator? Can un-freedom or slavery policy be sustained with no long-term ramification?)

Verse 81

和大怨 必有余怨 焉可以为善 是以圣人执左介 而不以责于人
故 有德司介 无德司彻 夫天道无亲 恒与善人

When big hatred is settled, there will always be residual hatred. (*Many Chinese are still angry with the Japanese because of the World War II invasion and the refusal of current Japanese government to express repentance. Some people just refuse to do the right thing. It only helps to unite the Chinese people in some ways. Although the Chinese people in general do not hate the innocent young Japanese and have no thirst for vengeance, there will always be some prejudice until the wartime documentaries and movies cease to be shown again due to lack of public interest.*) In this sense, how can a settlement of hatred considered perfect? Hence, great leader will hold the proof of debt but never press the debtors for repayment. (*A good leader should be munificent to lend helping hand to the citizens as well as the people of all nations, forgive the debts wherever possible. Repay hatred with benevolence. War breeds war, peace breeds prosperity.*) Therefore, the benevolent officer administers proof of debt; the unforgiving officer administers tax collection. The Nature has no preferential love; it always provides for the needs of all people. (*God has already given us everything we need for both our natural and spiritual life; some are just not delivered to our doorstep.*)

CONCLUDING REMARKS

Doing no intervention doesn't mean one doesn't care. It is like parents watching their adult children but do nothing, absolutely nothing, unless there is something to do. Have faith in them and give them total freedom to make good decisions as well as bad ones. Just because we have the just cause doesn't mean we have the rights and responsibilities to impose our desires on our children. We must not try to be clever and assume we know which way to go because there is a chance we may be pushing them in the wrong direction but we are overconfident to overlook the obvious. Step aside and trust in nature, life will find a way. Multiple young brains will be more powerful than one old brain, unless the young are not properly educated to deprecate intellectual subjects. Let them find the best way for themselves although some mistakes are inevitable but necessary and rewarding. Keep quiet, don't meddle around with their lives, and you will be loved.

Many problems are created due to human desires to unify the thinking of everybody; to have control over the organization for personal political objective or "presumed" public interest; to impose one's morality on others due to narcissism and bloated self-confidence; to create order by making thousands of rules which limit the freedom of the people; to have unwarranted development according to one's perception of beautiful and ugly; to achieve perfection; to have glorious name; and to have massive wealth to fund lavish lifestyle or to feel more superior to others. Very often problems are created for trying to solve problem which doesn't exist. It doesn't end well most of the time. The root cause is human desires. To correct this weakness, we must pursue no ambitious objective, do no intervention, and aspire for no sense of success or pleasure. Be contented with life and grateful to Mother-nature for what we have instead of focusing on what we lack.

Compassion feeling towards families and friends is natural in human as well as animals. There is no need to promote it like a rare commodity. Otherwise, even tulip can become more expensive than gold. Treating virtuous values with undue valuation will make some people pretend to be very religious to gain respect and access to the power centers. On the other hand, people who crave for virtuous showings will be deceived by pretentious virtues. A society which is very compassionate is no better than one which needs no benevolence because it means everybody is self-sufficient, financially and morally. Out of self-interest, we will naturally love others in order to be loved. But we must never expect others to reciprocate. What goes around comes around. We will eventually enjoy the self-interest of living in a benevolent society.

We should celebrate diversity instead of unity. Uniting around a leader is a symptom of moral bankruptcy. We need to aggressively challenge the conventional wisdom; seek out genuinely different ways of looking at things and perspectives that challenge what we may have accepted as being the truth. The education system must not inculcate obedience but encourage self-independence. We must not make "becoming rich" the objective of education. Instead, it is utmost important to give "freedom of the mind" to our children. They will then be able to resist pseudo-intellectuals from biasing them into seeing reality as being divided in the preference of the interest groups. Teach them to be contented with life and they will be able to live a happy and meaningful life regardless of their social status. Nobody can beat down their morale and they will not become a burden to society.

Darwin's Theory of Evolution or Natural Selection suggested that survival in the struggle for life is determined by the ability to adapt and live in harmony with the environment; as opposed to the best physical shape. What is more adaptable to environment than water? Soft like water can be more superior to rigidity. Take no confrontational stand; tolerate annoyance wherever possible, so long as it does not infringe on our freedom. Have war with no nations; buy peace in exchange for bilateral trade; prepare for war but negotiate for peace.

BIBLIOGRAPHY

Chen, Guying 陈鼓应著，老子注译及评介，中华书局，1984.

Xu, Kangsheng 许抗生著，帛书老子注译与研究，浙江人民出版社，1985.

Yi, Zhong Tian 易中天，先秦诸子百家争鸣，上海文艺出版社，2009.

Star, Jonathan, Tao Te Ching, Tarcher Cornerstone Edition, 2008.

Hansen, Chad, Laozi Tao Te Ching on the Art of Harmony, Duncan Baird Publishers, 2009

Griffith, Samuel B., Sun Tzu: The Art of War, Oxford University Press, 1971

AUTHOR BIOGRAPHY

Chung Boon Kuan (born November 22, 1967) is a professor at Universiti Tunku Abdul Rahman, Malaysia. He holds an electrical engineering degree and a PhD specializes in Electromagnetic Theory and Applications. He has a passion in Chinese philosophies which include the works of Lao Zi, Zhuang Zi, Confucius, Sun Zi, etc.; and Chinese history from 1000 B.C. to the 20th century; the world history; and economics. He has read many books related to these topics for more than 20 years. He likes to think of himself as a global citizen more than a Malaysian. He wants a better world. He believes the world will be better if politicians stop assuming they are clever enough to meddle around in the lives of the people and the world for good reasons. It is equally important for the people to firmly say no to any government interventions. Giving more power to the government means asking ultimately for more compulsion and less freedom.

READER REVIEWS

"Professor Chung is one of the few authors who have given a different perspective to original ideas of Lao Zi given in Tao Te Jing. Tao Te Jing is a book on philosophy of governance. For example, verse 31 is talking about the danger of having military forces but yet various authors tried to portray Tao Te Jing as a book on spiritual philosophy or even religious bible. Based on the philosophy of Lao Zi, Professor Chung is trying to give his views that everybody has to educate himself, become self-reliant instead of being fooled into complete dependency on a leader and choose freedom over being protected within a cell."—Professor Chuah Hean Teik, President of Universiti Tunku Abdul Rahman, Malaysia

"Many of us have not realized that Taoism is very different from Taoist teachings founded by Lao Zi. In Taoism, Lao Zi is popularly regarded as a god. Ironically Taoist teaching taught by Lao Zi is explicitly an atheist philosophy which is meant to guide us through the treacherous paths in life. This invaluable set of knowledge is encrypted in classical Chinese which is not easily interpreted by an average Chinese reader. In our Malaysian society most of us are better versed in English than Chinese. Professor BK Chung has recognized this setback and with his magnanimous heart, he has taken a lot of pain translating this Chinese script into English, and supplemented with many real-life examples to demonstrate the aptness of Taoist teachings in modern context."—Lim Hock Seng

"Our minds, known to us, are not wise but full with defiled thoughts. We have very little idea about our true minds. Tao Te Jing helps us to realize our true minds. This can be achieved by letting go all our conventional ideas, definitions, knowledge, and names. Shortly speaking, we have to let go all our thoughts. All the points highlighted in Tao Te Jing are helping and telling us to detach all the thoughts including the Way (Tao) and Names (Ming)."—Associate Professor Lim Yun Seng, Universiti Tunku Abdul Rahman, Malaysia